Businesses in Crisis: Learning from Good and Bad Management Decisions

By

Sally B. Acton, Jessica Alvarado, Steven D. Booker, Carl C. Caver, Eugene L. Cottingham, Timothy R. Jones, Crystal M. Kent, Jesse M. McCarthy, Michele A. Murphy, Kevin S. Suddeth

authorHOUSE®

AuthorHouse™
1663 Liberty Drive
Bloomington, IN 47403
www.authorhouse.com
Phone: 1 (800) 839-8640

This book is a work of non-fiction.

Published by AuthorHouse 10/26/2015

ISBN: 978-1-4184-3211-9 (sc)

Library of Congress Control Number: 2004095129

Print information available on the last page.

This book is printed on acid-free paper.

Acknowledgments

The Master of Science in Management Class # 65 at Oakland City University-Bedford would like to thank the faculty and staff of Oakland City University for providing us the opportunity, guidance, and facilities for completion of our Masters Degrees.

In particular, we would like to thank Pat Sharp and Ruth Norman for their support and guidance. We would also like to acknowledge each instructor for the individual experiences and knowledge they shared, while allowing us to express our own thoughts and experiences.

Our experience culminated with visits to Crane Division, Naval Surface Warfare Center, 1ˢᵗBooks Publishing, and Dunn Memorial Hospital. We wish to express our gratitude to the management and staff at each organization for providing excellent examples of management in action.

We would like to thank our families and friends who supported us during this 18-month adventure of frustrations and successes, as well as for their support and understanding of our commitment to further our education.

Our class, consisting of ten individuals from different backgrounds, worked as one unit to complete the Master of Science course work and to prepare this book. Sally Acton, Jessica Alvarado, Carl Caver, Steve Booker, Eugene Cottingham, Tim Jones, Crystal Kent, Jesse McCarthy, Michele Murphy and Kevin Suddeth contributed their own unique section to the book. Steve, Crystal, and Michele, our project editors, worked tirelessly and excelled at bringing this project together.

Student leadership for our MSM class has come from various sources and members at different times with no one person standing out. Tim, Steve, Crystal, and Kevin provided organizational leadership. Sally and Michele provided moral guidance and nurturing. Eugene, Carl, and Jesse contributed life experience. Keeping all of us in line was Jessica, who provided a humanitarian viewpoint throughout the course.

The Adult Degree program at OCU-B should be commended for offering the accelerated Master's degree program, which provides a flexible learning environment for working professionals. A heartfelt thank you from all of us!

Abstract

Organizations in the 21st century continue to learn from business failures that were the result of bad managerial decision-making, unethical business decisions, and/or dysfunctional business models. It is critical for leaders to understand the nature of the problems caused by bad business decisions that can produce disastrous results and ultimately lead to business failures.

This book outlines various situations of organizations in crisis and the tools management needs to recover from such situations. This book discusses functions of management that are critical to the success of an organization. In addition, examples are provided throughout the book of businesses in crisis and how we can learn from their good and bad management decisions.

TABLE OF CONTENTS

CHAPTER

ONE

From Industry to Information:

The New Revolution

A revolution is defined as "a dramatic change in ideas or practice." Revolutions are constantly happening within the business environment, and for that reason it is important that business leaders are able to adapt and look for ways to change. Just as the advent of new industrial processes forced businesses to alter their operations, today's leaders have to pay attention to the technological/informational revolution that is currently underway.

"The U.S. Department of Commerce has also released statistics, which document the increasing impact of eBusiness on our lives. The online sales figures for the third quarter indicate that total online retail sales reached nearly $6.4 billion for the quarter ended Sept. 30. That's a 15.3 percent increase from the previous quarter, and the biggest increase since the department started tracking eCommerce numbers a year ago" (Saik, n.d.).

Most companies understand the need for a strong technology infrastructure in today's marketplace. Those who choose to ignore the trends of today and do not look for the trends of tomorrow will be left behind.

Introduction

The last fifty years has witnessed a shift in internal management procedures, brought on by a new revolution – the Information Revolution. Some companies have recognized the need to meet these changing demands within the marketplace and have excelled by doing so. However, other companies have ignored the need to meet the challenges of the 21st century and suffered the consequences.

This chapter will focus primarily on how history has affected the practice of business today. There is no doubt that the Industrial and Information Revolutions have made a dynamic impact on how organizations now make decisions and how organizations will continue to make decisions in the future.

Industrial Revolution

In the eighteenth century, England led the Industrial Revolution as it initiated manufacturing practices to combat vanishing natural resources (Business Wire, 2000). The Industrial Revolution led to increased inventions, and manufacturing eventually spread from the Western world to the East. It was a time of dramatic change, from hand tools and handmade items, to products that were mass-produced by machinery (Business Wire, 2000). Workers became more productive, and since more items were manufactured, prices dropped, making exclusive and hard-to-make items available to the poor, as well as the rich and elite (Business Wire, 2000). Life generally improved, but the Industrial Revolution also proved harmful. Pollution increased, working conditions were harmful, and women and young children were forced to work long and hard hours (Business Wire, 2000).

The effects of the Industrial Revolution played a huge role in how business is conducted in today's society. Working conditions have been greatly improved and many problems that existed during the Industrial Revolution have been resolved with policies and laws. The Environmental Protection Agency and the Occupational Safety and Health Administration are two agencies that enforce these laws. In addition, labor unions were formed to promote communication between employees and managers, resulting in increased safety and equality in the workplace.

Information Revolution

Today's challenge is the impact of the Information Revolution, which is just beginning to be felt (Business Wire, 2000). Like the Industrial Revolution, the Information Revolution is a time of drastic change. Today's society is constantly affected by the technology that is fueling the Information Revolution. It is not only information or the effect of computers and data processing that fuels this impact on decision-making, policymaking, and strategy as discussed in Business Wire (2000):

> The impact is felt most from something that very few anticipated or talked about ten or fifteen years ago: e-commerce -- that is, the explosive emergence of the Internet as a major, perhaps eventually the major, worldwide distribution channel for goods, for services, and, surprisingly, for managerial and professional jobs.

This effect is profoundly changing economies, markets, and industry structures; products and services and their flow; consumer segmentation, consumer values, and consumer behavior, as well as jobs and labor markets. However, the impact may be even greater on societies and politics and, above all, on the way we see the world and ourselves in it (Business Wire, 2000).

Businesses are seeking new ways to use the Internet to create real-world value (Business Wire, 2001). "Take any manufacturing firm in a vertical industry and you will notice the need to bridge the gap between product and distribution" (Business Wire, 2000). In the old-school manufacturing supply chain, the distributor held the power. However, manufacturers realize that the possibility of Internet-powered distribution through multiple channels, and even direct consumer sales, gives them greater control (Keough, 2002). This new information business model allows the consumer to order directly from the manufacturer, but the distributor still packs and ships the goods. "This allows the distributor to take greater care for the consumer since they spend less time taking orders" (Keough, 2002).

Today, this business model demonstrates why many businesses are successful and others have failed. Kmart's strategy in the year 2000 was to buy through wholesalers rather than buy direct – three-step versus two-step (Wirebach, 2002). Kmart's competitors chose another route, as detailed in this response by Wirebach (2002), "Remember, Wal-Mart doesn't deal with middlemen. It only deals directly with the suppliers that can cut the price." There was "no way" Kmart could compete with Wal-Mart without buying direct.

The Industrial Revolution, when the goal was to provide massive amounts of goods by manufacturing at low prices, is long gone. Today's Information Revolution requires attention, strategy, and competitive gain. The challenge is to use the technologies of today to effectively and efficiently disseminate information transfer, while improving processes and gaining business value.

The companies that are not integrating e-commerce into their long-term strategic planning are falling far behind. Many dot-coms have fallen behind as well, but they did not have a business model to follow that represented a long-term strategy. Many dot-coms failed to see the consumer and jumped into the consumer web without conducting marketing studies (Keough, 2002).

One consulting firm, Sherwood Partners, was asked by Keough, an author for the Los Angeles Business Journal, "Why did so many of the Web's grand ideas fail" (Keough, 2002)? Sherwood Partners replied that it had a client who invested 50 million dollars into a dot-com without surveying potential customers; it assumed it would have a large customer base. When asked if they thought their dot-com was going to work, the employees said "absolutely," without first doing a survey to find their customer's base needs (Keough, 2002).

The Importance of Managing Information Technology

In subsequent chapters of this book, many examples of failing organizational systems will be discussed. In many instances, these failures are due to a lack of communication. How do business leaders fail to communicate effectively, given the accessibility to today's high tech communication tools? Information technology is our greatest tool, but how an organization integrates, values, and utilizes these tools, which are necessary to conduct business in today's current practice, must now be a part of strategic planning. An old cliché says, "A carpenter is only as good as his tools." In the same context, a business is only as good as its communication tools.

This is very true in the health care field, as illustrated by the following quote from Business Wire (2001):

> Historically, provider organizations have under-invested in technology, but the right system can improve an organization's financial outlook through streamlined operations, efficient workflow, and assisting in business decision-making…When looking for a technology vendor, provider groups should look for two important factors – experts in managed care business processes and technical expertise to build a technology infrastructure that seamlessly integrates vital administrative and management functions.

During the Industrial Revolution, the tools to make goods improved and evolved into manufacturing machines. In today's Information Revolution, the structure has changed dramatically. Computer resources, or information technologies, have become the tools necessary to govern, translate, and disseminate data for all types of resources and machinery. This allows data to be readily available for decision-making.

It is paramount for business leaders to understand that communication in the Information Revolution takes place with human resources, and human resources utilize machines in an organized, fast-paced, and useful manner. During the Industrial Revolution, machinery was manually maintained and there was not a system available in which to manage the amount of failures and part malfunctions. Today, businesses have the technology and the information management to make that data readily available.

What manufacturing was to the Industrial Revolution, information technology is to the Information Revolution. What does this mean? The Industrial Revolution lasted over 200 years. Will the Information Revolution last that long? If it does, we should be preparing for flexibility. Modernism has increased the level of information flow and businesses are learning to manage information for an ever-changing system of technology that will require long-term strategic planning.

In the technology market, the primary asset is the people, says a manager from a software design company. He proceeds to say that the secondary asset for any software driven business is the source code, the hardware designs, patents, and web sites. Successful businesses are technology savvy and know their priorities (Keough, 2002). Understanding technology is, therefore, a critical strategy. One example is today's wireless technology future. Marty Pichinson, of Sherwood Partners states:

> It is not even a question if wireless technology is the future. AT&T, I think, made a major, major mistake by selling off its wireless. You go to Sweden and you can buy a soda from a vending machine with your cell phone. AT&T's decision to get out of wireless was short-term (Keough, 2002).

The Importance of Utilizing Information

Technology allows business leaders to have the data available to make effective short and long-term decisions. However, when management does not utilize this gold mine of information, business suffers.

The plunge Kmart has taken since 2000 deals with some strategic short-term decisions that damaged the Kmart reputation. "For a long time, Kmart could never decide if it was in or out of the automotive business. It never fit the Kmart target customer – the busy-budget housewife" (Business Wire, 2001). A basic marketing strategy is to 'know thy self' with a competitive business model, then, know the consumer's needs and wants.

Another well-known corporation, whose mistakes we can learn from, is Levi Strauss:

> With roots dating back to the mid-19th century gold rush era, Levi Strauss, a company closely held by four descendants of its namesake founding father, had long set the industry standard for the five pocket jean and its rugged authenticity, whether worn by farmers in the 1800s, factory workers in the 1930s, or James Dean-styled rebels (Dolbow, 2000).

In the 1950s, Levi elevated the blue jean to the status of a cultural icon. But in the 1990s, the brand lost ground to mainstream and designer labels that held more allure for the fickle youth market (Dolbow, 2000).

Levi Strauss failed to keep up with fashion trends and changing times. Levi Strauss lost billions as it watched the hems and cuffs of its competitors' jeans grow. Levi's sales shrank from a high of $7.1billion in 1996 to $5.1 billion in 1999 (Dolbow, 2000). The problem was something that a trend analysis could have brought to the forefront. A strategy was needed to understand the market's push towards the latest styles: cargo pants, large baggy pants, and bell-bottom low-rise styles that the competitors market targeted for ages 18-24 (Dolbow, 2000).

In 2003, Levi Strauss was a different story because of hard work and its strategy to implement new lines of jeans that targeted 18-24 year olds. According to Business Wire (2003), Levi Strauss has turned things around and "net income in the third quarter of 2003 was $27 million compared to $14 million for the same period last year, an increase of 95 percent."

Business Wire (2003) attributes this amazing turnaround to the strategy of networking through 3,000 Wal-Mart stores all over the nation to promote a new line of Levi jeans. This strategy has improved sales domestically, as well as in Asian countries.

Today, Kmart and many dot-coms still struggle, while successful companies such as Gap, Nike, and Wal-Mart continue to use the right strategies to stay ahead. How do organizations that were once successful pull themselves out of the crisis and create an effective and successful organization? The answer is more than a business mission statement; it is the ability of an organization to recognize that times change, and to insure survival, a business must also be prepared to adapt to those changes.

<u>Conclusion</u>

The Industrial Revolution has given organizations the ability to become more dynamic and efficient. The Information Revolution and information technology will be the guide to truly revolutionize the success or failure of organizations in the 21st century. It is the management of information that guides decision-making, organizational communication, financial and marketing management, globalization, business policy, and strategic planning. Enhancing the world around us for a greater civilization through business technologies will help claim or reclaim the successful future of many organizations.

Businesses can recover from a crisis by learning from historical practices and gaining knowledge to rebuild organizational success. The following chapters in this book can guide managers into the 21st century business model with an integrated historical account of organizational decision-making that has led to success and failure within many major corporations.

References

Dolbow, S. (2000, November). Assessing Levi's patch job. *Brandweek*. Retrieved May, 2003 from http://www.findarticles.com/cf_0/m0BDW/43_41/67160375/print.jhtml

Business Wire. (2000, October 25). Industrial Revolution meets the Information Revolution. Retrieved May, 2003 from http://www.findarticles.com/cf_0/m0EIN/2000_Oct_25/66321747/print.jhtml

Business Wire. (2001, November 12). Ten things provider organizations can do to improve financial performance. Retrieved May, 2003 from http://www.findarticles.com/cf_0/m0EIN/2001_Nov_12/79954135/print.jhtml

Business Wire. (2003, September). Levi Strauss & Co. announces third-quarter 2003 financial results. Retrieved May, 2003 from http://www.findarticles.com/cf_0/m0EIN/2003_Sept_30/108300902/p1/article.jhtml

Keough, C. (2002, May). Mopping up: after reviving music careers, Marty Pichinson turned to businesses--helping ease the pain for failing dot-coms and offering survival tips to those still going. *Los Angeles Business Journal*. Retrieved May, 2003 from http://www.findarticles.com/cf_0/m5072/18_24/91091739/print.jhtml

Saik, R. (n.d.). The future of eCommerce. Retrieved May, 2003 from http://www.iboost.com/profit/articles/20024c.htm

Wirebach, J. (2002, March). How the Big K crumbled: Kmart's descent, Penske ties could shake up the aftermarket. *Aftermarket Business*. Retrieved May, 2003 from http://www.aftermarketbusiness.com/aftermarketbusiness/article/articleDetail.jsp?id=12078

CHAPTER

TWO

Technology:

Management for Effective

Communication & Decision-

Making

When a company views its Information Technology (IT) as just another overhead expense, it is making a fatal mistake. A firm's technology is one of its greatest assets. Effective decision-making demands accurate and timely information, as well as smooth communication. To be competitive, it is necessary to be flexible, move quickly, meet customer demands, integrate operations, and increase market share. In today's business world, all of this is being accomplished via IT.

When a company is in trouble financially, competitively, or otherwise, decisions have to be made quickly and precisely. The level of technology infrastructure that is available to the leaders within a corporation could mean the difference between making the correct decision or floundering for too long and allowing the competitors to gain ground or even pass your company by. So, how do you view IT? Is it just another expense or is it one of your company's greatest assets? You will find out how to increase your IT infrastructure and why it is important to do so as you read this chapter.

Introduction

The first chapter showed how important the impact of the Information Revolution has been, and will continue to be for effective business operations. Recovery from an organizational predicament demands that information technology solutions be established immediately and executed flawlessly. This technology must lend itself to total communication among all the players in the business environment and it should aid managers in making the crucial decisions needed to recover and excel.

This chapter will discuss several key points to consider when planning and implementing an information system for effective decision-making. To elaborate the need for effective information systems, this chapter will also give examples of implementation procedures and corrections of faulty information systems.

Organizational Decision-making

Decision-making can be intuitive; it can also be gained from information on paper, computer, or film records. The primary objective in using information in decision-making is using valid and current information. This has become more difficult in the last decade because there is more information available. There are two fundamental causes for the increased information flow. The first cause is modernism, created from new complex organizations replacing the old "mom and pop" businesses. The second cause derives from a growth in democratic government policies, such as monitoring program expenditures and operations.

A critical part of information technology, which aids in decision-making capabilities, is record storage. Record storage can be in someone's head, on paper, on microfilm, or on a computer. The actual storage of records can change for a number of reasons: it can change when the volume of information increases, it can change from a paper environment to one that is paperless, or it can remain untouched if needed for historical or archival purposes. The main reasons to go paperless are that it is less costly and gives greater utility to the decision maker. Information is an important resource, which if properly managed, can lead to improved decisions and greater productivity.

The Problem of Rising Costs

One key point to consider is that information costs are rising. Society's capability to produce more and more information is contributing to this cost. One way to cut costs in information technology is to improve the information systems. Philip Hutchens (n.d.) writes:

> There are ten steps for improving an information management system. They are: 1) Establish control over the creation and use of new information by using an analyst to take an active role in the establishment or revision of a data collection system. This analyst may want to become involved in the actual steps or procedures involved; 2) Treat information management as a management function by limiting the establishment of a data collection system to those which are needed for sound policy decisions; 3) Eliminate unnecessary records; 4) Insure systematic maintenance and disposal of information by using legal time frames for destroying old records; 5) Provide for the proper selection, effective utilization and control of office equipment; conduct in-depth studies of duplicating and quick-copy requirements and costs; 6) Control computer output; solve paperwork problems with computers by eliminating reports, reducing the size of reports by delivering only summaries, or preparing only deviations from prescribed norms; 7) Instruct staff to filter or combine related paperwork; 8) Control promotional propaganda paperwork; 9) Contact public officials – the Office of Management and Budget (OMB) is an excellent source of protest regarding Federal information collection requirements); and 10) Don't review information just because you might be asked about it.

Another way to offset information technology cost involves the use of virtual teams. According to Townsend, DeMarie, & Hendrickson (1998, p. 17-29):

This concept is cost-effective and allows flexibility throughout the organization. Additionally, firms benefit from virtual teams through access to previously unavailable expertise, enhanced cross-functional interaction, and the use of systems that improve the quality of the virtual team's work.

Virtual teams are possible because of recent advances in computer and telecommunications technology. Three main technologies that define the infrastructure of virtual teamwork are desktop videoconferencing systems (DVCS); collaborative software systems; and Internet/Intranet systems"(Fasser, Yefin, & Vrettner, 2002, p. 153).

Once an organization has established a need for virtual teams, the next challenge is to put them in place. At this point, the organization must define each team, function and organizational role, develop the technical systems to support the teams, and assemble individual teams, as well as a cross-section of potential team workers.

Understanding System Frameworks

In order to be able to implement necessary changes in any type of system, there must be an understanding of the frameworks of the system. First, it is important to know the key elements of an information technology system. In an information management system, information is processed in many ways for effective decision-making, including: classifying of data, rearranging/sorting data, summarizing data, performing calculations on data, or selecting data. Jennifer Rowely (1998) writes:

> There are four distinct levels in an information framework. These are the information environment, information context, information system, and the information retrieval. The information environment is the environment that surrounds the information contexts; it consists of political, legal, regulatory, societal, economic, and technological forces. The information contexts are the contexts in which information systems are encountered. Organizations and businesses are an important category of context, but other contexts are also possible, including education, home, and the community. Information systems are systems designed to enter information, store it, and facilitate effective retrieval. Systems include hardware, software, data, and in some cases, users. Information retrieval is concerned with the individual interfacing with a system or range of systems, or sources with a view to meeting specific conscious or unconscious information requests. It concerns the actions, methods, and procedures for recovering information from stored data.

Another framework to discuss is the actual information technology procurement process. This framework is made up of two processes—the deployment process and the management process. Robert Heckman (1999) outlines these in the following manner:

> The deployment process consists of requirements determination, acquisition, contract fulfillment, supplier management, and quality management.
> Requirements determination…may include: organizing project teams, using cost-benefit analysis to justify investments, defining alternatives, assessing risks and benefits, defining specifications, or obtaining the necessary approvals to proceed with the procurement process.
> Acquisition…may include identification of sourcing alternatives, generating communication to suppliers, evaluating supplier proposals, or negotiating contracts with suppliers.
> Contract fulfillment…may include expedition of orders, acceptance of products or services, installation of systems, contract administration, and management of post-installation services such as warranties or maintenance, or the disposal of obsolete equipment.

> Supplier management...may include development of a supplier portfolio strategy, development of relationship strategies for key suppliers, assessing and influencing supplier performance, and managing communication with suppliers.
>
> Asset management...may include activities such as development of asset management strategies and policies, development and maintenance of asset management information systems, evaluation of the life cycle cost of IT asset ownership and management of asset redeployment and disposal policies.
>
> Quality management...includes activities such as product testing, statistical process control, acceptance testing, quality reviews with suppliers, and facility audits.

The management process guides the overall IT procurement process. It consists mainly of supplier management, asset management, and quality management.

There are several concerns with the IT procurement management process. These include how to make the procurement process more efficient, the search for reliable and valid ways to evaluate and assess performance, ways to create effective working relationships, ability to plan to develop an effective procurement strategy, legal problems, the financial and total cost of ownership, and obtaining executive support for the procurement manager's activities.

There are a few action items a procurement manager might implement to improve the process. Robert Heckman (1999) writes that they are:

> 1) Develop IT procurement performance metrics and use them to benchmark the IT procurement process; 2) Clarify roles in the procurement process to build effective internal and external relationships; 3) Use the procurement process framework as a tool to assist in reengineering the IT procurement process; 4) Use the framework as a guide for future research: and 5) Use the framework to structure IT procurement training and education. This five-item agenda provides a foundation for the professionalization of the IT procurement discipline. As the acquisition of information resources becomes more market-oriented and less a function of internal development, the role of the IT professional will change necessarily.

The Cost Benefits Analysis for Information Technology Needs

It has never been an easy task to achieve buy-in for new equipment purchases from the decision makers. In the information technology world, this remains true. It is imperative to be able to document your case for new purchases to those who will make the decision. For this reason, it is necessary to discuss some analytical techniques involved in the cost benefit analysis and how these might help sway the decision makers to purchase the new technology.

The cost benefit analysis is one tool used to acquire approval for a purchase within a company. The term is defined as simply as it sounds; it is an analysis of the costs compared to the benefits of an action. The business case web site (located at http://www.solutionmatrix.com/) provides a coherent study of some of the components involved in a cost benefit analysis. A cost benefit analysis can include one or more of several different approaches.

For instance, one may choose to include a Return on Investment (ROI) analysis, which measures the gains of an investment over its costs. ROI is projecting expected profits, then taking the difference between the projected profits and the costs, and dividing this number by the total costs. The assumption is that the alternative with the highest percentage of ROI is the choice to make. Sometimes, however, other more complicated ratios are also referred to as Return on Investment. These could include return on capital, return on total assets, and return on equity. Because of this complication, it is imperative that all decision makers involved have a clearly defined idea of what the ROI analysis will include. They must also understand the limitations of such an analysis, which include not factoring in risks, or properly matching returns with the cost that bring those returns.

Another approach to the cost benefit analysis is to use a financial justification. A financial justification needs to take into consideration the needs and the situation of a business at that point in time. Is the business working with little cash flow? Is the business focusing on profit, or is quality a more important factor at the time? Financial justification depends simply on the needs and priorities of the company. IT personnel should focus their justification on this aspect. One should ensure every benefit of the proposed system is assigned a monetary value.

Lastly, approaching the cost benefit analysis with the idea of the Total Cost of Ownership (TCO) can be an essential factor in the decision as well. This is especially true of IT purchases where the cost of owning a piece of equipment could be many times more than the investment costs, which is almost always true. A TCO analysis will bring out buried costs not initially apparent such as repairs and maintenance, insurance, and licensing. The business case web site mentioned earlier provides a useful matrix that examines all the resources involved compared to the system life cycle (acquisition, operation, and future growth). This is another analysis that should be used when all other factors in the decision-making process are equal and the only difference is cost. A comparison of the TCO for all alternatives should be presented to develop a full picture for the decision makers.

Cost benefit analysis can be as financially simple or as complicated as the decision makers require in approving the new system. The level of importance of the new system might lead one to determine the amount of detail s/he includes in the analysis. On the web site listed earlier, there is a short paper by the president of the company entitled, "The IT Business Case: Keys to Accuracy and Credibility." From this paper one can either learn what to expect from an IT business case or how to write and present one.

Strategic Planning for Information Technology

As with any type of business plan, an information systems plan must include, on some level, a strategic plan. As Marks (2002, p. 352-353) says:

> Having defined its purpose, vision, mission, and core values, the [IT management team] must have a great strategy to close the gap between where [they] are and where [they] want to be. Creating a strategy that raises the [information system of a company] up to a higher, more competitive level is the leadership's responsibility.

It is important that a company be able to evolve. Survival of the fittest relies as much, if not more, on a company's information technology system as it does on other areas of the business. If a company, and specifically its IT system, is not growing and evolving, it is most likely dying. This type of evolution has been referred to as the 'Principle of Information Darwinism.' According to Marks (2002, p. 10), this concept:

> Addresses how firms view IT, as a strategic weapon or as a budgetary necessity. It concerns how corporations invest in IT, at minimal levels…or as an option, a financial investment that will provide superior returns over time. The firms that view IT as an expense and their IT department as an overhead expenditure will not survive the next wave of change.

Dell Computer is an example of a firm that is based on an information-intensive mode of competition. IBM, Hewlett-Packard, and many other PC manufacturers that covet one of its key internal benefits — its negative working capital business model – envy Dell's make-to-order manufacturing model. Dell orders components for its products only after the customers have paid for them in advance. In other words, Dell receives the order information from its customers, as well as payment in advance, and then purchases the inventory to make the product and ship it. This approach is the reverse of most manufacturing companies, which forecast demand for product, purchase inventory in advance using their own working capital, and manufacture and ship the product to distributors, wholesalers, and eventually retailers, who sell them to end customers. Dell has replaced the need for inventory with information. Dell's mode of operation is as much based on information management skills as manufacturing asset management skills (Marks, 2002). It is also important to note that:

> Executives who recognize the value of IT in today's business environment and leverage it as a strategic weapon will be the survivors. Their firms will win more market share, retain more customer loyalty, and demonstrate superior financial performance because of choosing IT as one of their main competitive weapons. (Marks, 2002, p. 17)

Marks (2002. p. 195) also writes, "Survive and compete are the two evolutionary processes of a firm that are primarily focused on short-term viability."

Now let us shift our discussion to the future-oriented evolutionary activities of a firm, which are replication and adaptation. No company can endure in a competitive environment with only short-term initiatives; it is always important to have a strategic plan that looks toward future activities:

> Replicate initiatives focus on reinventing efforts to reposition a company for… a new business environment or a new technology paradigm. Adapt initiatives focus on how a firm positions itself for multiple futures, largely unknown and longer term. Replication and adaptation initiatives require the same process as survival and competitive initiatives: analysis of change capabilities. (Marks, 2002, p. 213)

One way to manage technological change is by using the strategic partnership approach. This partnership requires a specific strategy in order to be effective. "A strategic partnership for the management of technological change is a goal-focused collaboration involving two or more parties operating with equal influence and mutual respect, in which they jointly plan each step of the innovation process" (Haddad, 2002, p. 29).

"The first step in strategic planning is generally an internal and external environmental scan" (Haddad, 2002, p.22-23). One effective method for doing an environmental scan of the company's information technology is to use the SWOT (Strengths, Weaknesses, Opportunities, and Threats) analysis, in which the company analyzes itself in these areas.

If your information system management team does not already have a mission statement, it is imperative to develop one. "This statement is an articulation of how the business, agency, or educational institution views itself, and what it aspires to be" (Haddad, 2002, p. 23). Once this mission statement is in place, goals can easily be identified. "From an organization or department's goals flow specific business objectives and strategies for meeting them, and this is the third step in strategic planning" (Haddad, 2002, p. 26).

After goals and objectives are identified, the necessary technology and investment strategy can be developed. "The selection decision may be whether to develop the technology in-house or purchase it from an outside vendor" (Haddad, 2002, p. 26). Given that no information technology system can go forward without the end user, it is also crucial to "establish procedures for end-user input on technology design features and specifications" (Haddad, 2002, p. 26).

"The fifth step in strategic technology planning is to measure the organization's readiness for modernization. This latter activity may be done through a survey tool, structured interviews, or a combination of the two" (Haddad, 2002, p. 26). If the IT team concludes from these measures that the company or end-users are not yet ready, it is nevertheless worthy to keep in mind that evolution is necessary for survival. More training for end-users or better justification to upper management may be in order; even going back to the drawing board is an alternative, but giving up should rarely be an option.

Haddad (2002, p. 27) states:

> The final, sixth step in the strategic planning process is for the strategic planning committee to put forward an action plan for achieving the goals, objectives, and strategies. This action plan should have a precise time frame and specific, achievable milestones at incremental steps of the progression
> Strategic planning for technology acquisition helps to ensure that the technology will in fact advance the organization's mission and business objectives and not be based merely on a vendor's recommendation or an executive officer's infatuation. The other piece is partnership.

Implementing and Correcting Information Systems

Following are three examples of actual hands-on activities involved with the implementation process or correction of an IT system. Each example illustrates the need for information technology system planning. It can be done, but all the bases must be covered.

To begin with, let us discuss Otis Elevator in Bloomington, Indiana. This company moved to an IT system dictated by its parent company, a relatively common occurrence when two businesses merge. IT personnel thought there could be a smooth transition by simply moving the old system into the new system. However, most of the end-users had stand-alone systems that were not part of the overall system. When the new system was brought online, it immediately crashed because the IT team had failed to properly plan for the transition. Several IT team members were terminated because of this failure. New managers were brought in and they incorporated a task force to communicate with all end-users to avoid a repeat of the first transition failure. All of the personal computer systems were integrated into the big picture, and when it was re-implemented, it passed with flying colors (E. Cottingham, personal communication, July 15, 2003).

A second example involves Dunn Memorial Hospital in Bedford, Indiana. Some time ago, an information system was purchased for use in the hospital. The cost was substantial; however, no one could use the system to its full potential because the end-users lacked proper training. The system was becoming obsolete without contributing anything to the productivity of the hospital. The hospital was losing money, and the inefficient IT system contributed to this demise. Eventually, a new CEO was put in charge and began to rectify the situation. His expertise prompted him to assign a task force to address the system and bring back on board those that sold the hospital this system in the first place. The vendor was held accountable and eventually brought the system up to the standard it was supposed to be at in the first place. The process continues to improve, and the bottom line is reflecting the advances made in this endeavor (R. Wallace, personal communication, July 8, 2003).

The third example involves a company that has made vast improvements in the area of information technology. Bristol-Myers Squibb Company announced on March 18, 2003 the opening of a new research hub in Singapore, which will focus on helping its scientists collect important clinical data more rapidly in order to expedite development of new medicines. Bristol-Myers Squibb is able to do this because of a partnership with Platform Computing, which provides the resources to run scientific algorithms internally. Instead of running simulations of new drug compounds on expensive high-end computers, company scientists can route the same computations to desktops and laptops for process. Bristol-Myers believes it can increase its research computing power fivefold immediately and as much as a hundred-fold over the next few years as more personal computers are tapped. Every PC processor tied into the grid is employed full time. So far, there are thousands of computers tied to this grid (McCormick, 2002).

Bristol-Myers CIO, Ziff Davis, shares the effectiveness of this program by recalling the time he started out in pharmaceuticals. He states:

> When I first entered this industry, in the early 1980s, a good-sized pharmaceutical company would bring out hundreds of compounds, maybe a few thousand compounds from their drug discovery laboratories every year and test them. Five years ago, that number — might have been 10,000. Today, companies are synthesizing and testing 10,000 a day, hundreds of thousands a month" (Davis, n.d.).

Conclusion

In this chapter, it has been shown that technology has provided many tools and concepts to help get a business back on track. It is important to remember, though, that it takes strategic planning, wisdom, and intuitiveness to select the right combination of technology and processes, which will not only revive the company, but also allow it to excel.

References

Davis, Ziff. (n.d.) IT and pharmaceutical data: finding needles in haystacks. Retrieved March 27, 2003 from http://www.cioinsight.com/article2/0,3959,1152204,00.asp

Fasser, Yefin & Brettner, D. (2002). *Management for quality in high-technology enterprises.* New York: Wiley-Interscience.

Haddad, C. (2002). *Managing technological change: a strategic partnership approach.* Thousand Oaks, California: Sage Publications.

Heckman, R. (1999). *Managing the IT procurement process.* Boca Raton, Florida: CRC Press.

Hutchens, P. (n.d.). Information management and the decision maker. Unpublished article.

Marks, E. (2002). *Business Darwinism: evolve or dissolve: adaptive strategies for the information age.* New York: Wiley.

McCormick, J. (2002, November 11). Bristol-Meyers grid reveals new drugs. *Grid Today, 1.* Retrieved January 25, 2004, from http://www.gridtoday.com/02/1111/100700.html

Rowley, J. (1998). Towards a framework for information management. *International Journal of Information Management, 18,* 359 – 369.

Townsend, A., DeMarie, S., & Hendrickson, A. (1998). Virtual teams: technology and the workplace of the future. *Academy of Management Executive,* 12, 17-29.

CHAPTER

THREE

Critical Issues in Organizational

Communication

With all of the technological advancements we have made that help in the communication process, it is important to not forget that it is humans who are doing the communicating. Whether sending an e-mail, making a phone call, instant messaging, teleconferencing, video conferencing, or face-to-face, what we say and how we say it is still the most important factor in good communication. When was the last time your organization trained its staff in the art of communication? It is our hope that as a leader, you will discover the need to continuously find ways to improve this critical area of your business.

Introduction

As detailed in the last chapter "Technology: Management for Effective Communication and Decision-Making," technology has provided companies several tools that can be used to benefit the entire organization. This technology has enhanced the media used in communication. However, it is still in the hands of the individual to communicate effectively. Communication within an organization is comprised of individuals effectively expressing themselves. Managers set the tone and lead by example (whether they like it or not), so it is imperative that they be competent communicators.

This chapter will explore the dynamics of good communication and poor communication, the actual processes involved with communication in an organization, and what can be learned from the communication mistakes of others.

Technology and Communication

Technological advances have proven to be a positive factor in the ease and improvement of communication. At the same time, these advances have increased the complexity of communication:

> Technological growth has occurred rapidly in the last four years. Mathematics describes this development as an exponential increase. Instead of a gradual (slow) increase in technology, growth has skyrocketed. This growth results from inventors building upon the knowledge and improvements of other inventors. (Seymour, Ritz, & Cloghessy, 2000, p. 336)

No matter what type of technology is chosen, the communicators are still the individuals using the technology. Organizations must equally develop skills and technology in communicating. "Many researchers believe that the future in communication/information technology is only limited by the imagination. Microelectronics and computer technology have led to many of today's innovative products" (Seymour, et al., 2000, p. 338). Brna, Baker, Stenning, & Tiberghien (2002, p. 155-6) add:

> Computers are becoming increasingly important as tools for articulation and communicating information and technology. At the same time, theories in human learning strengthen the hypothesis that learning is an active process during which knowledge is constructed as opposed to just received via some communication channel.

Good Communication

One company discussed throughout this book is Bristol-Myers Squibb. In its long-range plans, Squibb plans to push communication. This objective was set forth in Squibb's Sustainability 2010 Goals presentation. The plan entails communication as the key for implementation of the company's goals. For Bristol-Myers Squibb, this is not just a good concept; research has already been conducted and action taken.

According to ClientPlus (2003), a consulting firm hired by Bristol-Myers Squibb, interpersonal communication is the life-blood of any organization. Despite the fact that everyone recognizes its importance, most failures are attributed to "poor communication." Communication is the single most important and most frequently misused leadership tool.

Business communication is becoming more challenging, especially in the new information age. One of the challenges facing business leaders is the increasing sophistication of communication tools. With the emergence of fax machines, voice-mail, e-mail, and teleconferencing, business managers are compelled to examine the costs and benefits of these tools to maximize their use. Bristol-Myers Squibb is no different.

Neil Katz & Associates (2004), also utilized by Bristol-Myers Squibb, provides consultation, training, and development services to businesses. Some of the major topics Neil Katz & Associates covers include communication skills in the workplace, leadership and learning, and mediation. Each of these deals primarily with communication.

By focusing on effective communication, management demonstrates it understands that:

Workplace relationships function as information-sharing, decision-making, influence-sharing, and emotional support systems. Healthy workplace relationships can increase employee satisfaction and commitment to the organization and can decrease turnover. Unhealthy relationships can affect the opposite outcomes. Thus, workplace relationships are important to both employees' work experience and organizational effectiveness. (Knapp & Doly, 2002, p. 615)

While it is sometimes necessary to communicate unsavory news, Otis Elevator Company showed good communication skills when it made an unpopular announcement. On Monday, August 27, 2001, Otis announced it would lay off 460 employees by the end of 2002. Although this announcement shocked many employees, it provided employees an opportunity to prepare for future employment. The initial announcement was followed by more specific communications that allowed employees to fine tune their job seeking plans.

On December 4, 2003, Otis Elevator again exemplified good communication skills in bringing bad news to its employees. The company announced that it planned to discontinue all factory, distribution, and field tool facility operations in Bloomington by the end of 2004. Otis' reason for this decision was due to significant changes in the global elevator market. Otis displayed integrity by giving employees ample notice about the factory shutting down. There have been several examples of employees from other companies going to work one morning, and at the end of the day, being told that their jobs were done and not to come back. Otis Elevator Company behaved in a much more professional manner by being up front with its employees and letting them know the bad news right away, giving them time to prepare for the future.

Poor Communication

Consider the following points, which give statistical and anecdotal information concerning the effects of communication:

A Louis Harris poll showed 93% of 230 primary care physicians agreed that better communication could help avoid serious medical problems. PHILCO Group, a major medical malpractice insurer, has data attributing as much as 70% of litigation, involving doctors, with poor communication.

Friction decreases productivity in all areas. Most managers spend at least 15 percent of their time (nine weeks per year!) dealing with 'personality squabbles' that good interpersonal communication skills and supporting communications could help mediate.

In the book, "Built to Last: Successful Habits of Visionary Companies," a common thread among companies that have been effective during their long histories is a habit of smart information-sharing and the consistent and effective communication of the culture and expectations of employees and managers. Examples of these are Nordstrom, the Walt Disney Company, Hewlett-Packard, 3M, Motorola, Boeing, and Proctor & Gamble.

In Levering and Moskowitz's "The 100 Best Companies to Work for in America (1994)," having open communication between management and employees is a key aspect of the culture of the highest-ranking companies.

According to research conducted by the International Association of Business Communicators Research Foundation, a clear majority of Chief Executive Officers deemed communication an integral – and often underutilized – contribution to effective, productive employees, company profitability, and successful corporate initiatives.

The Computer Security Institute found that information security breaches cost the 563 companies it surveyed more than $100 million in 1996. When employees do not have the information they need to help protect the company's proprietary information, the company loses on the best front-line defenses of information security.

Companies that survey managers and employees often find that well over half of managers felt they did not have the information or interpersonal communication skills they needed to make their staff members as productive as possible or meet their staff members' needs for critical information. (Ivy Sea Inc., 2004)

A new NASA report, "Enhancing Mission Success – A Framework for the Future," was recently released, authored by the space agency's chief engineer. Underscored in the 87-page document is the need to improve communication at all levels within NASA. "Failures in communication are an endemic problem that constantly threatens organizations, and particularly large complex organizations like NASA" (Griner & Keegan, 2000).

Factors involved with communication

According to Te'eni (2001, p. 252):

Nowadays, managers have at their disposal a wide variety of communication technologies from which to choose. A number of recent studies have reviewed and extended theories of how managers choose a medium for a specific situation. Nevertheless, current technology can also affect **what we communicate,** as well as **how we communicate it.** Thus, the question for designers has become broader: how should technology be designed to make communication more effective by changing not only the medium, but also attributes of the message itself?

In many instances, communication has three factors that are associated with it. These factors are inputs, processes, and impacts:

Inputs to the communication process: (1) task attributes, (2) distance between sender and receiver, and (3) values and norms of communication.

A communication cognitive-affective **process** that describes the choice of (1) one or more communication strategies, (2) the form of the message, and (3) the medium through which it is transmitted.

The communication **impact:** (1) the mutual understanding and (2) relationship between the sender and receiver. (Te'eni, 2001, p. 254-255)

Social Processes in Communication

Given that communication in organizations happens between humans no matter what media is used, managers should have a strong grasp of the social processes involved with good communication. Managers need to evaluate which social process a situation involves so they can effectively communicate the message. There are four broad social processes that require communication: reaching understanding, coordinating action, building relationships (socialization), and strategically influencing others.

"The simplest instance of reaching understanding is in *instructing action*, which has the goal of getting the receiver to act according to the sender's wishes" (Te'eni, 2001, p. 262-264). One of the many reasons that courage is an essential attribute in a manager is because it is sometimes necessary to give unwelcome directives. To reach understanding, it is imperative to have clear objectives, performance measurements, and incentives. "The aim of *managing interdependent action* is to coordinate interdependent actors" (Te'eni, 2001, p. 262-264).

As was discussed in the previous chapter, modern technology has provided the means for the development of virtual teams. Virtual teams have not eliminated the need for effective personal communication, as most teamwork is still done face-to-face. A manager can facilitate effective interpersonal skills by building powerful teams. A powerful team is composed of a variety of personalities rather than similar ones. A team with a leader and a lot of yes-men will not provide the opportunity for dynamic ideas and brainstorming. When coordinating a team, a cross-section of the company's personalities is needed. An example of such a team would include a leader, a rebel with a cause, a facilitator, a details person, a problem solver, and a challenger as well as multiple focused, hard workers.

"The purpose of *managing relationships* is to foster relationships between people at work" (Te'eni, 2001, p. 262-264). It is the manager's job to build, maintain, and facilitate good relationships. As Stephen Covey says in his book, "The Seven Habits of Highly Effective People," "Effective relationships are 100% your responsibility." A manager does not always agree with employees or coworkers, but managing relationships to achieve optimum results is necessary. Once the choice is made to make the relationship work, the possibilities for success are endless.

The manager will not sway opinions or achieve buy-in with his or her title and position alone:

> *Influencing* can be either action oriented or relationship oriented. Influencing is about attempting to influence behavior and attitude in order to conform to the sender's wishes but realizing the receiver can behave differently. Influencing is often concerned with resolving conflicts and, thus, it reflects high interdependence between communicators, more so than thinking collectively. Moreover, the need for influencing assumes a multiplicity of views or preferences held by the communicators, which need to be connected. (Te'eni, 2001, p. 262-264)

The Future of Communication

Globalization, competition, technological sophistication, and speed have increased the complexity of organizations. Clearly, communication should enable organizations to cope with such complexity. Underlying this approach is the realization that new forms of communication and new forms of organizations are being encountered everyday:

> Enterprises of the future are likely to rely even more heavily on virtual organization. Trust will be crucial. At the same time, however, they may find it more difficult to develop trust between people who hardly ever meet. Thus, communication is expected to play a growing role in promoting not only task-oriented goals, but also relationship-oriented ones. (Te'eni, 2001, p. 298-299)

Conclusion

Technology is very important to an organization, but the level of communication skills is what determines whether a business will succeed or fail. This chapter has looked at effective communication strategies and examples of poor communication. As the statistics cited earlier show, there have been tremendous advances in technological communication, but there is still a long way to go to achieve effective communication. Communication sometimes turns into the game 'telephone,' where someone relays information to someone else and as it goes from person to person, the information changes dramatically. Perhaps even with all the modern marvels now in existence, such as e-mail, the Internet, and video conferencing, the result will still be the same. Business leaders must continually educate themselves and their employees to be effective communicators. In a recent Verizon Wireless commercial, the actor keeps asking, "Can you hear me now?" Most people hear, but do they truly listen? It takes ongoing training to insure that good communication becomes a way of life within an organization. The future of the company depends on it.

References

Brna, P., Baker, M., Stenning, K., & Tiberghien, A. (2002). *The role of communication in learning to model*. Mahwah, New Jersey: Lawrence Erlbaum Associates.

Griner, C., & Keegan, W.B. (December 18, 2000). Enhancing mission success – a framework for the future. Retrieved from http://www.nasawatch.com/fbc/12.21.00.NIAT.pdf

ClientPlus. Communication. Retrieved January 18, 2003 from http://www.clientplus.com/fintimes/topics/topics_display.cfm?topic_id=163

Ivy Sea, Inc. (2004). Making the case for good communication. Retrieved from http://www.ivysea.com/pages/ct0799_1.html

Neil Katz and Associates. (2004). Retrieved from http://www.mediationworks.com/mti/ct/katz.htm

Knapp, M. & Doly, J. (2002). *Handbook of interpersonal communication*. Thousand Oaks, CA: Saga Publications.

Seymour, R., Ritz, J., & Cloghessy, F. (2000). *Exploring communication*. Tinley Park, Illinois: The Goodhart-Willcox Company, Inc.

Te'eni, D. (2001, June). Organization communication and IT. *MIS Quarterly, 25.*

CHAPTER

FOUR

Financial Management and

Recovery

Recent headlines are filled with the financial mistakes, misleadings, and misrepresentations of organizations. The businesses involved, the families of the employees who lost their jobs, the stock market, federal laws, and even the economy, have been affected by these events. Seemingly strong, growing, profitable companies are folding in on themselves. When one reads the headlines about these companies, it becomes startlingly clear that improvements in corporate America, especially where finances are concerned, are necessary. This chapter will outline critical areas within finance that are particularly in need of enhancement. Specific examples will be pulled from the headlines of recent history to illustrate what can go wrong financially and how it can be avoided.

Introduction

Finances play a major role in any company and proper financial management is one key to keeping a company on strong ground. This fact has been illustrated in the downfall of many prestigious corporations in recent years. Critical areas of finance that led to these failures include poor financial controls, inaccurate accountability, and weak leadership by the Chief Financial Officer (CFO) and other upper-management.

Companies such as Qwest Communications and Bristol-Myers Squibb are two companies that have encountered these types of problems. A company afflicted with one or more of these problems is going to have a more difficult time recovering from a crisis than one with sound financial practices. A successful road to recovery must begin with a strong foundation in financial management, which starts with financial controls. This chapter will be covering the aspects of sound financial leadership and the role that leadership plays in the overall success or failure of a company. Two companies whose financial struggles played a major role in the crisis encountered by them will be analyzed.

Financial Controls

With the recent fraudulent findings of accounting practices performed in companies such as Arthur Andersen and Enron, accounting rules and standards have become more intensely scrutinized. Bazerman, Loewenstein, and Moore (2002) state that even though accounting may seem objective, there are many areas that are very subjective. Some of these areas include when to recognize revenue, when to record expenses, and what an appropriate depreciation schedule might be for the company. Many financial issues are left up to individual interpretations and all of these interpretations fall upon the financial department. The responsibilities of a company's financial department can be difficult to grasp, and increased scrutiny will bring even more accounting controls to ensure the truthfulness of a company's financial statements.

CFO Leadership

Hiring a CFO with a proven record of accomplishment of leading a company in a positive direction is vital to good financial management. This person must lead with integrity to decrease the risk of fraud. The CFO of a company has many areas to manage in order to lead the company in a promising direction. A company needs a CFO who is knowledgeable in all areas of financial management, including asset and debt management, budgeting, investing, and forecasting future growth.

A significant responsibility of a CFO is the preparation of accurate financial statements for presentation to the owners of the company. To accomplish this task, the CFO must follow the standards outlined by the Generally Accepted Accounting Principles (GAAP), which are set by the Financial Accounting Standards Board (FASB). If these guidelines are followed, the presentation of reliable financial statements will not be a problem.

Hiring reputable auditors will insure the truthfulness of financial statements. The auditing firm needs to probe the reasoning behind any questionable bookings of revenue and expenses, even at the risk of antagonizing the client. The auditor must thoroughly investigate accounting procedures and policies, report any inaccuracies found, and provide an unbiased opinion. If any of these are not accomplished, the possibility of misleading shareholders is increased.

The concept of corporations employing auditors is not without fault. How can an auditing firm question the judgment of the financial department when, in a sense, the company employs the auditor (Bazerman, Loewenstein & Moore, 2002)? If an auditing firm gives a company an undesirable opinion, it is at risk of losing a client. This is not an issue in companies led with integrity and honesty, which allows for the unbiased opinion of the auditors.

Throughout the late 1990's, business was booming for most sectors of the economy. However, light has recently been shed on the reasons why some corporations were able to report strong profits. A few of these companies misrepresented their financial information with improper bookings of items such as sales, expenses, and depreciation. Following are two examples of companies that failed to adhere to proper financial management and went through Securities and Exchange Commission (SEC) investigations. It is important to study crises such as these to learn from the mistakes that can result from improper financial management.

Qwest Communications

Qwest is an international company that provides telecommunication services to over 30 million customers in the U.S. and abroad. Its services include internet-based data, voice, and image communications (Qwest.com, 2003). A local exchange carrier owned by Qwest provides the company with 85% of its revenue and 90% of its profits. Qwest also has operations based in foreign countries.

Qwest is a utility company regulated by the Federal Communications Commission (FCC). With regulation by a government agency, it might seem that improper accounting would be almost impossible. This company, however, managed to overstate revenues for the years 1999 through 2001. The recent findings of improper accounting will force Qwest to restate its earnings for those periods. Fundamentally, the company has some issues with its finances besides the restatement.

Looking back at the years ended 2000 and 2001, this company did not present favorable numbers. In 2000, Qwest reported revenues of $16.61 billion, but the deductions of expenses resulted in a net loss of $810 million. A contributing factor to the net loss may have been the acquisition of U.S. West, a telephone company based out of Denver (Qwest.com, 2003). By purchasing U.S. West, Qwest was able to increase its area of service, but the acquisition significantly increased its debt.

The following year did not improve much for the company. Revenues were reported as $19.69 billion for 2001, but once again, the company achieved a net loss, this time in the amount of $3.96 billion. Besides reporting a net loss for these two years, the company has some issues that will need to be addressed if it wants to survive these tough years. Compared to industry averages, Qwest under performs in many areas, as shown in Table 1 ("Qwest Financial," 2003).

Qwest's inability to record sales in a timely manner is an underlying issue to the restatement (Martin, 2002). An example of this is the booking of capacity contracts. The SEC is looking into whether the company booked these contracts as one lump sum, rather than recognizing the revenue over the life of the contract (Martin, 2002). With these improper recordings of revenues, Qwest portrayed a better financial standing than really existed. In order to insure these irregularities do not occur again, Qwest and its shareholders need to demand integrity and honesty in the company's financial department. If Qwest can avoid these problems, the company has a better chance of overcoming the issues at hand.

Table 1. Financial Snapshot of Qwest Compared to Industry

Financial Strength	Company	Industry	Sector	S&P 500
Quick Ratio (MRQ)	0.74	0.85	0.80	1.17
Current Ratio (MRQ)	0.83	1.03	1.35	1.69
LT Debt to Equity (MRQ)	NM	1.72	0.87	0.74
Total Debt to Equity (MRQ)	NM	1.92	0.98	0.98
Interest Coverage (TTM)	-10.22	3.77	7.07	11.30
Management Effectiveness (%)				
Return On Assets (TTM)	-32.16	2.69	5.74	6.34
Return On Assets - 5 Yr. Avg.	-5.16	4.03	5.71	7.57
Return On Investment (TTM)	-36.87	3.55	7.78	10.25
Return On Investment - 5 Yr. Avg.	-5.77	5.57	8.29	12.14
Return On Equity (TTM)	-98.39	9.12	12.92	18.45
Return On Equity - 5 Yr. Avg.	38.58	18.33	15.19	21.03

Being a publicly traded company, Qwest is required to have its financial statements audited each year. During the years in question for the company's financials, Qwest employed Arthur Andersen as its auditing firm. Andersen should have been able to detect the improper recordings if a thorough and complete audit had been conducted. The company took a step in the right direction in the year 2002. Qwest released Arthur Andersen of its duties and hired KPMG as its new auditing firm (Martin, 2002). Given the chance to reevaluate Qwest's financial statements of Qwest, KMPG found other areas that were not recorded correctly. As a result, the company announced in February, 2003 that the restatement of revenues would rise from the previous amount of $1.16 billion to $2.2 billion (Qwest.com, 2003).

Another area of concern with Qwest is the amount of both long-term and short-term debt the company is carrying. Before any restatements, in 2002 Qwest had $26.5 billion in debt on its books. The event of restating revenues will increase the amount of debt, causing an already debt-ridden company to become even more so (Martin, 2002). At this time, the future does not look bright for this company.

If Qwest cannot correct the issues it faces, there may be no other option than filing for bankruptcy and reorganizing. A few policies Qwest may want to implement in order to rise above this disaster is to, first, improve customer service. With an improvement in this department, the company may have an opportunity to increase revenues with the sale of more products. Secondly, Qwest may want to decrease its amount of debt. One answer may be to sell off some of its debt, or the sale of assets to pay off this debt may be another option (Martin, 2002). Lastly, the company may want to change the way it records revenues and expenses. This may be accomplished through conservative accounting practices and by following GAAP and the standards set by the FASB. If Qwest does not correct these issues, the company may not be able to overcome the disaster it has faced since the first overstatement of revenues in 1999.

Bristol-Myers Squibb

Bristol-Myers Squibb (BMS) is a pharmaceutical company founded in 1887. Some of the company's major medical products include: Pravachol, used in the prevention of coronary heart disease and secondary prevention of cardiovascular events; Plavix, a platelet inhibitor; and HIV/AIDS therapy Sustiva ("Bristol-Myers," 2003). BMS is another company that is heavily regulated by government agencies. Like Qwest, BMS also had a restatement of earnings for the years 1999 through 2001. Financially, this company is much sounder than Qwest, but the restatement involves similar issues. Since the stock market slide in 2000, drug companies have outperformed the broader market. Bristol has not been one of these companies, as shown in Table 2 (Revell, 2003). Three major events helped contribute to the downfall of this company.

Table 2. Bristol-Myers Squibb Financial Snapshot Compared to Industry

Growth Rates (%)	Company	Industry	Sector	S&P 500
Sales (MRQ) vs. Qtr. 1 Yr. Ago	0.82	6.10	13.96	8.39
Sales (TTM) vs. TTM 1 Yr. Ago	-0.39	6.45	13.26	4.15
Sales – 5 Yr. Growth Rate	3.78	9.78	15.30	9.98
EPS (MRQ) vs. Qtr. 1 Yr. Ago	-70.79	27.87	36.40	24.56
EPS (TTM) vs. TTM 1 Yr. Ago	-91.87	23.62	27.73	24.08
EPS - 5 Yr. Growth Rate	-5.79	12.96	16.69	10.60
Capital Spending - 5 Yr. Growth Rate	11.22	14.50	6.11	-0.85
Valuation Ratios				
P/E Ratio (TTM)	122.69	21.59	23.95	23.34
P/E High - Last 5 Yrs.	48.40	59.72	62.38	49.97
P/E Low - Last 5 Yrs.	19.27	20.86	21.47	16.64
Beta	0.50	0.48	0.56	1.00
Price to Sales (TTM)	2.40	4.36	5.39	3.07
Price to Book (MRQ)	4.70	7.82	6.78	4.45

First, the company lost about $2 billion in sales during 2002 (Revell, 2003). This accounts for about 11% of the company's revenue, and a large part of that was the loss of patents on three major drugs: Taxol a cancer medicine; Glucophage, a diabetes drug; and BuSpar, an anti-anxiety medicine. The loss of these patents resulted in a significant hit to revenues. Other drug companies can now produce forms of these medicines, causing BMS to look elsewhere for sources of revenue.

Second, the loss of these revenues resulted in an investment in ImClone Systems, a biotech company (Revell, 2003). ImClone was supposed to create the next big cancer drug, Erbitux. BMS invested approximately $1.2 billion for a stake in ImClone, but the investment did not work out as planned. The Federal Drug Administration (FDA) delayed the Erbitux go-ahead, causing the emergence of other issues (Revell, 2003). ImClone founder Sam Waksal, as well as lifestyle guru Martha Stewart, were involved in an insider-trading scandal, which resulted in indictments against them.

Third, the SEC and the United States Department of Justice launched investigations into BMS's inventory and accounting practices. This was a result of the company participating in a practice known as "channel stuffing" (Revell, 2003). Bristol persuaded its wholesale customers to purchase an additional $2 billion worth of drugs than they actually needed in 2001, so the company could meet earnings targets for 2001 (Revell, 2003). The effect of these actions caused the company's sales to drop dramatically in

2002, since the wholesalers already had inventory. All of this was part of the March 2003 restatement affecting the years 1999 through 2001. The company lowered sales in these years, which subsequently caused sales for 2002 and 2003 to increase. The timing in the recognition of these sales was the issue that caused the restatement.

BMS may be able to overcome these obstacles based on experience and changes in management and accounting practices. Having been in business since the late 1800's, BMS has been through all cycles of a business, so it should be able to draw on its experience and apply it to today's issues.

In addition, BMS may want to increase the amount invested in research and development. A recent study shows the company below industry standards in R&D. The average drug company has a market capitalization equal to $5.39 for every R&D dollar it spends on its longer-term drug pipeline. The market credits BMS with only $3.30 in market capitalization (Revell, 2003). With an increase in this area, the company may be able to recapture some of the revenues lost due to the loss of major drug patents. Every dollar invested in this area creates a better chance of bringing a breakthrough drug to the market.

Bristol may also change current accounting practices in order to avoid such issues in the future. As discussed with Qwest, if GAAP and the standards set by the FASB had been followed, the company might not have faced some of these dilemmas in 2002 and 2003. In the short-run, shareholder maximization was accomplished, but the long-term implications may not have been accounted for from the start. In an era of short-term performance, long-term profits are sometimes sacrificed. Therefore, Bristol may need to change both accounting and management practices to achieve more complete shareholder wealth maximization.

Conclusion

Bringing a company back into 'the black' can be a very daunting task, and having a strong foundation in the financial department is a good start. This starts with quality leadership and proper procedures to ensure accurate financial statements. The CFO sets the standards the employees will follow when making key financial decisions. Implementing the standards set by GAAP and the FASB may assist in the correct recording of items such as revenue and expense. In addition, employing a thorough and competent audit firm will support the presentation of a solid financial standing.

A company on the verge of failure may need to analyze all areas of the company, but identifying exactly what strengths and weaknesses are held within the finance department may be the first step to restoration. Building on what the company does well, and correcting what is done wrong are key to the whole recovery process. Both Qwest and Bristol-Myers Squibb are prime examples of companies that need to closely monitor all financial decisions. If correct accounting standards had been followed, these two companies might have been able to avoid some of the issues that they faced in the last five years. In addition, Qwest and Bristol might have been able to avoid further problems if quality financial decisions had been made. As stated earlier, finances play a major role in any company, and the proper management of these finances is a guide to keeping a company on strong ground.

References

Bazerman, M., Loewenstein, G., & Moore, D. (2002, November). Why good accountants do bad audits. *Harvard Business Review, 11*, 96-103.

Bristol-Myers Squibb Company Profile. (2003). Retrieved March 23, 2003, from http://www.finance. yahoo.com

Martin, M. (2002, August). Qwest sinks deeper into trouble. *NetworkWorld, 33.*

Qwest financial snapshot. Retrieved March 2003 from http://yahoo.investor.reuters.com/StockOverview. aspx?country=US&ticker=Q&coname=QWEST+COMMUNICATIONS+INT.&mxid=1000628 46&target=/stocks/quickinfo/stockoverview&cotype=1&page=default

Qwest accounting errors worse than thought. (2003, February). *Computergram Weekly, 2.*

Qwest Company Profile. (2003). Retrieved on March 23, 2003 from http://www.qwest.com

Revell, J. (2003, February). Bristol-Myers cleans up its mess. *Fortune.* 147, 78-101.

CHAPTER

FIVE

The Significance of Business

Ethics

Every company would like to think it is following ethical guidelines. There are times, though, when a situation is not even recognized as unethical until it is too late. There are also times when a situation is recognized as unethical but not illegal. Then there are those who know that what they are doing is both unethical and illegal, but do it anyway. As a member of management, it is imperative to understand what ethics are, what situations might call for closer scrutiny of the decisions made, and how to make ethical decisions.

Those coming out of business schools to become today's leaders will, in many cases, have more ethics training than ever before. For now, those who are already in leadership positions could benefit from implementing best practices in business ethics. Unfortunately, ethics are not the first thing to come to mind when one thinks about managing a company. This chapter can help leaders focus on the subject with practical solutions and examples.

Introduction

"A quick glance at recent headlines in the Wall Street Journal, USA Today, or the local daily newspaper immediately reveals that business ethics – or the lack thereof – is not only a hot topic in the mass media, but also a subject of daily discussion for millions of working Americans" (Ferrell & Gardiner, 1991, p. xi). Today, many businesses are in serious financial trouble and their leaders are being sent to prison because of the unethical business decisions they choose to make. This is not a new dilemma in business, but more business leaders are being caught and punished than ever before.

Lower level managers and employees face situations every day in the workplace that are unethical, illegal, or both. They must decide how best to handle these situations and weigh the potential consequences of their decisions. They must calculate the risk of stepping forward or of keeping silent, as well as the chance of being fired, reprimanded, demoted, having a promotion withheld, or even being arrested.

This chapter will discuss what business ethics are and provide a general list of ethical issues that cause leaders to make tough choices every day. Examples will be given of companies whose leaders are in serious trouble for making unethical business decisions, as well as an example of a business that prides itself on outstanding ethical behavior. Finally, this chapter will discuss ways in which leaders can become more ethical and the reasons why leaders need to be more ethical.

What Are Ethics?

It is important to remember that a company's reputation is based on the image the public has of that company:

> One of the most important factors in a company's image is the way its employees treat its customers and clients as well as the general public. The way a company treats its own employees is another important factor in corporate image. A positive corporate image creates respect and confidence in the company and its products or service. More and more people determine where they want to work and with whom they wish to do business based on corporate ethics. (Jaderstrom, Kruk, & Miller, 2002, p. 119 – 120)

Jaderstrom et al. (2002, p. 119) proceed to state:

> The most successful people and companies are those who behave ethically. The leaders of a corporation set the tone for ethical behavior, and this determines how employees, customers, and competitors are treated. Ethical problems in business are not just a matter of knowing right from wrong, but involve looking at business questions from a reasonable, responsible, and consistent point of view.

The first item to consider is the definition of ethics. According to Ferrell and Gardiner (1991, p. 2), "An ethical act or decision is something judged as proper or acceptable based on some standard of right and wrong." Ethics includes both legal and moral aspects. According to Jaderstrom et al (2002, p. 119):

> The legality of an action is determined by law. The morality of an action is determined by ethical rules of right and wrong. Ethical behavior requires following the spirit as well as the letter of the law. An ethical business follows rules and trusts that other businesses and their employees will do the same, despite the fact that some unscrupulous business people take advantage of this trust.
>
> Employees may behave unethically because they do what they are told to do without considering the consequences. They may be afraid of losing their jobs, or may not understand management expectations. The corporate climate determines employee behavior. For example, when there are slack internal controls, employees may feel free to use work computers for personal reasons or to make an excessive number of personal telephone calls. Employees may be asked to tell "white lies" to protect their supervisors. On the other hand, when management treats employees as trustworthy adults, employees are more likely to act responsibly.

Ferrell and Gardiner (1991) believe that two additional criteria are needed to help people make ethical decisions in the workplace. First, an ethical act is one that leads to the greatest benefit for the most people, and second, one that increases the self-esteem and mental health of the person engaging in that act. Ferrell and Gardiner (1991, p. 34-35) state:

> Many of the tough choices we face in the workplace relate to problems, situations, or controversies in which we must choose among several actions, which may be judged by others as right or wrong (whether we like it or not). These choices often develop from conflicts between an individual's personal moral standards and the strategies, policies, or values of the organization in which he or she works. It is often difficult to discern when a "promotional incentive" becomes a bribe, for example, or to recognize when an advertisement is deceptive or to know how much puffery can go into a sales presentation.

> Many of the tough choices we face are decisions that will affect others both inside and outside the organization. In general, most businesses seem to be overly concerned with ethical issues that could damage their reputations. Such companies try to avoid scandals and front-page news coverage of incidents that appear to damage them or their products.

Ferrell and Gardiner (1991, p. 35-36) sort these tough choices into four categories of ethical issues. They are as follows:

> *Conflicts of interest* - When a person is faced with the tough choice of deciding whether to advance his or her own personal interests or those of the organization, a conflict of interest exists. For example, in North America it is usually accepted that employees should not accept bribes, personal payments, gifts, or special favors; people who do so are often placing their own interests ahead of those of their employer, as well as those of competitors and consumers. For example, when a real estate developer who just happens to serve as a director of the hometown savings and loan association, obtains especially favorable financing for a project from that same S&L, he has placed his personal interests ahead of those of the S&L, as well as other customers of the S&L. Customers may question why he has received such a good deal when they have not; others may question whether the deal was in the best interest of the depositors. These days, such questions are often followed by calls from Congressional investigators.

> *Honesty and Fairness* - The terms honesty and fairness have universal appeal and business people are expected to follow these principles as well as all applicable laws and regulations. When businesses knowingly harm customers, clients, employees, or competitors through deception, misrepresentation, or coercion, however, they are acting in their own self-interest and violating these basic principles. More importantly, when these principles are violated, it destroys trust and makes it difficult, if not downright impossible, to conduct business.

> *Communications* – Some of the tough choices that arise in the workplace involve honesty in personal memos and daily conversations with others in the organization. Other issues include deception in advertising messages and lying in communications with other government or regulatory organizations. In fact, lying is a major ethical issue in business today. Once again, lying and deceptive communications create ethical issues because they destroy trust and complicate business transactions.

> *Organizational Relationships* – Tough choices in organizational relationships concern how people in the organization relate to customers, suppliers, employees, co-workers, and others. Some of these choices include whether to disclose confidential information obtained from others (like the boss's secretary), how to meet obligations and responsibilities, how to avoid unduly pressuring others and possibly encouraging

them to behave unethically, and whether to take someone else's work and present it as one's own without providing credit or compensation. How often is a strategic plan or report simply copied, with a quick change of name, and passed on as original work?

Ferrell and Gardiner (1991) understand that making ethical choices in business can be troublesome because business ethics is not simply an extension of an individual's personal ethics. Most decisions in a given situation involve some degree of conflict and it is not always obvious or easy to identify what is the right or correct choice. "Few of us always make the best decision, but the more informed we are, and especially the more quickly we recognize an ethical issue, the more likely we are to have an opportunity to resolve it successfully and ethically" (Ferrell & Gardiner, 1991, p. 36).

All workers bear the responsibility of ethical behavior in the workplace every day, especially the leaders at the top of an organization whose decisions can make or break a company. The bottom line is that the majority of working people must rely on the leaders in their organizations to make business decisions that will benefit as many people as possible, not just themselves, and that will not bring harm to the company.

However, many business leaders, past and present, make decisions that seem to be helping only a few people at the top, and in the long run, are harming a lot of innocent people who were not even involved in the decision-making process. Ferrell and Gardiner (1991, p.1-2) state:

> The late 1980s were a Waterloo for ethical behavior in American business. Arbitrageur Ivan Boesky was jailed for insider trading. Junk bond king Michael Milken was sentenced to ten years in prison after being convicted of conspiracy and various securities fraud-related charges. American consumers were conned out of billions of dollars through telephone sales of worthless stocks and phony oil leases. In the early 1990s, a Congressional hearing uncovered fraud and deception in American savings and loan associations. Insider trading and bribery in business were widespread. Various surveys showed that business students in college at that time were less ethical than their counterparts already working in the real world. Lying, cheating, and stealing seemed to be acceptable business practices.

Examples of Unethical Businesses

Unfortunately, these business practices have continued into the new millennium. Many business leaders are under scrutiny for unethical and illegal business decisions and some have already been sentenced to serve time in prison. Companies such as Enron, Arthur Andersen, and WorldCom have endured major financial losses due to the inappropriate and greedy decisions made by their leaders. "The Justice Department is conducting a criminal investigation of Enron Corp., focusing on whether former executives of the Houston energy trader manipulated its profits to inflate the company's stock prices and deceive investors" (Johnson & Behr, 2003, par.1).

Authorities have so far indicted former Chief Financial Officer Andrew Fastow and former Enron treasurer Ben Glisan and both have been sentenced to prison terms. "In its indictments of Glisan and Fastow, the government contended that personal greed was a driving motive in the secretive off-the-books deals they created" (Johnson & Behr, 2003, par. 4). More indictments are expected in the Enron case.

As briefly discussed in chapter four, Arthur Andersen is another company in serious trouble because of unethical business decisions that were made by its leaders:

> Arthur Andersen served as Enron's sole auditor throughout the energy giant's sixteen years. The SEC questioned Arthur Anderson's inaccurate audit statements and Enron's overstated profits...The SEC and several congressional committees continue to investigate whether or not Arthur Andersen compromised its professional ethics or violated accounting standards set by the GAAP. (MacNeil & Lehrer, 2002, par. 1,3,7)

Further, it was stated:

The SEC has also fined the firm $7 million for improper professional conduct with other companies, including overstating client Waste Management's earnings by $1.4 billion. In June, 2002, a federal jury convicted Arthur Andersen of obstruction of justice by destroying Enron-related materials to impede an investigation by securities regulators. The accounting firm told the SEC it would cease auditing public companies by August 31, 2002. (MacNeil & Lehrer, 2002, par. 8 & 9)

MacNeil and Lehrer (Sept 2002, par. 1) later reported that:

> Prosecutors say David Myers [former World Com CFO] and Scott Sullivan, former Chief Financial Officer at WorldCom, instructed employees to hide more than $3.8 billion in expenses on balance sheets, allowing the telecommunications company to increase its reported profits when in actuality, it was losing money.

Myers is cooperating with authorities, which could put pressure on Sullivan to make a deal with prosecutors and tell them if WorldCom CEO Bernie Ebbers was aware of the falsified accounting. Myers was sentenced on December 26, 2002.

Another example of a recent ethical scandal is Boeing Company. In December 2003, Boeing's Chairman and CEO Philip M. Condit, resigned amid allegations of unethical behavior at his company. As reported in Business Week ("The Fallen Managers," Jan 12, 2004), several ethical scandals were occurring at Boeing under Condit's leadership. The CFO at Boeing was fired for allegedly offering a job to an Air Force procurement officer during a contract negotiation, and in July 2003 Boeing was punished for "possessing 35,000 pages of stolen documents from rival Lockheed Martin Corp. Boeing has been banned from bidding on military satellite launches, and the Pentagon has transferred contracts worth $1 billion to Lockheed" (p. 77). Though Condit may not have been personally responsible for these scandals, it is the responsibility of any company's leadership to instill ethical behavior in its employees to insure it does not become the next Boeing, Arthur Andersen, or Enron.

Example of an Ethical Business

Even though there are many companies that are participating in unethical behavior, there are companies who do take pride in their high ethical standards. Armstrong World Industries is one of these companies. It was founded in1860 and originally worked on the principle of caveat emptor, "Let the buyer beware." However, in 1864, owner Thomas Armstrong adopted the motto, "Let the buyer have faith," and put his own name on every product. Today, Armstrong World Industries is a major manufacturer of floor coverings and building products with sales in the billions of dollars.

However, even companies who have strongly established ethical values have to maintain the organizational commitment to them. As Aguilar (1994, p. 72) says, "The job of corporate ethics is never quite finished." William Adams, chairman and president of Armstrong World Industries observed, "A company's ethical conduct is something like a big flywheel. It might have a lot of momentum, but it will eventually slow down and stop unless you add energy" (Aguilar, 1994, p. 72). When asked how Armstrong sustains its ethical climate, Adams responded:

> We reinforce our commitment to ethical practice in several ways. First, we talk about ethics all the time. Second, the company has an explicit statement of principles to guide us in our actions. Third, we make sure to check on performance. Fourth, we punish the violators. Fifth, we give all our people the opportunity to talk to anyone in the company in connection with concerns about ethical issues. Access to the top people can be very important. (Aguilar, 1994, p. 73)

Additions to Adams' list by other managers were the kind of people hired, successive presiding officers having the same high values, and working hard to remove temptations. Promoting the company's high ethical standards and discouraging misconduct are ways in which Armstrong World Industries keeps the ethical flywheel turning and keeps the motivation going to sustain these high standards.

How to Become More Ethical and Why this is Important

It seems that more companies need to adopt the high ethical standards of companies like Armstrong World Industries. The business world may be in serious trouble if it continues on its current trend. What can be done to ensure that business leaders try harder to make more ethical business decisions? According to Blanchard and Peale (1988, p. 26), a leader should ask him or herself these questions before making a business decision: "Is it legal, is it balanced, and how will it make me feel about myself?" Blanchard and Peale (1988, p. 80) also list the "Five Principles of Ethical Power for Individuals" that they feel business leaders should follow:

> *Purpose*: I see myself as being an ethically sound person. I let my conscience be my guide. No matter what happens, I am always able to face the mirror, look myself straight in the eye, and feel good about myself.
>
> *Pride*: I feel good about myself. I don't need the acceptance of other people to feel important. A balanced self-esteem keeps my ego and by desire to be accepted from influencing my decisions.
>
> *Patience*: I believe that things will eventually work out well. I don't need everything to happen right now. I am at peace with what comes my way!
>
> *Persistence*: I stick to my purpose, especially when it seems inconvenient to do so! My behavior is consistent with my intentions. As Churchill said, "Never! Never! Never! Never! Give up!"
>
> *Perspective*: I take time to enter each day quietly in a mood of reflection. This helps me to get myself focused and allows me to listen to my inner self and to see things more clearly.

By following these principles, Blanchard and Peale (1988) believe that a leader will be better equipped to make ethical and sound business decisions. In the end, a leader will be able to feel good about the decisions s/he made and will keep the company and him or herself out of legal and financial trouble.

Business schools are becoming concerned about the lack of ethics being displayed by today's business leaders:

> With so many aspects of the corporate culture suddenly thrown under the ethical microscope, administrators of MBA programs find themselves reconsidering the depth and breadth of their ethics curricula… "Certainly the events of the past year with Enron have raised awareness of the importance of these issues in the public's mind," said Verna Monson, director of student life at the Carlson School of Management at the University of Minnesota, Minneapolis. "Our students say it is important, and employers also say it is important. Employers are looking for…competent managers but for managers who can be leaders in the area of ethics." (Stone, 2002, par. 6 & 9)

To address the demand, the school has started some programs that deal with the issue of ethics in business. Other schools, such as Villanova University, Drexel University, and Temple University are also implementing more classes on business ethics (Stone, 2002).

The federal government is also trying to ensure that business leaders are following better business practices. "In a signing ceremony in the East Room of the White House, President Bush enacted new legislation that toughens penalties for corporate fraud, establishes an independent accounting board, and increases spending for the Securities and Exchange Commission" (MacNeil & Lehrer, July 2002, par.1). The President stated:

> These are the most far-reaching reforms of American business practices since the Depression and the bill will send a strong message urging corporate America to uphold their responsibilities or they will be exposed and punished. The legislation quadruples the maximum jail time for corporate executives and auditors indicted for wire or mail fraud, setting sentences at 20 years. The bill also classifies securities fraud as a crime that could carry a prison sentence of up to 25 years…A new independent board will

oversee the accounting industry, which largely had been monitored by members of its own profession. Following the indictment of Enron auditors Arthur Andersen, the accounting self-regulatory system has come under pressure to reform. (MacNeil & Lehrer, July 2002, par. 2 – 4)

Conclusion

Corporate leaders must take a new look at their commitment to business ethics. "The practice of business ethics and compliance has evolved dramatically over the last decade, and if a company has not kept up with advances in the field it may be among those embroiled in tomorrow's scandals" (Petry, 2002, par. 1). Petry (2002, par. 7 & 8) goes on to say:

> If a corporate leader chooses not to address business ethics, he or she is increasing the risk of fines, penalties, the cost of litigation, the loss of reputation, and the defection of investors. Taking a new look at a company's commitment to business ethics is not only the smart thing to do in terms of a corporate leader's job security, it is also the right and necessary thing to do. Today, there is no more critical responsibility for corporate leaders that to affirm that their organizations have kept up with business ethics best practices, are fully aware of recent developments, and are doing everything that can be done to act in accordance with the highest standards of ethics, integrity, and compliance.

References

Aguilar, F. (1994). *Managing corporate ethics.* New York: Oxford University Press, Inc.

Blanchard, K., & Peale, N. (1988). *The power of ethical management.* New York:
    William Morrow and Company, Inc.

The Fallen Managers. (2004, January 12). *Business Week.* p. 76.

Ferrell, O., & Gardiner, G. (1991). *In pursuit of ethics.* Springfield. IL: Smith
    Collins Company.

Jaderstrom, S., Kruk, L., & Miller, J. (2002). *Complete office handbook (3rd ed.).* New York: Random
    House, Inc.

Johnson, C., & Behr, P. (2003, September). Enron probe focusing on executives' motives. Retrieved
    September 15, 2003 from http://www.washingtonpost.com/ac2/wp-dyn/A51556-2003Sep9?langu
    age=printer

MacNeil & Lehrer, (2002). Arthur Anderson, LLP. Retrieved September 15, 2003, from http://www.pbs.
    org/newshour/bb/business/enron/player6.html

MacNeil & Lehrer, (2002, July). President Bush signs corporate reform bill. Retrieved September 15,
    2003, from http://www.pbs.org/newshour/updates/bush_07-30-02.html

MacNeil & Lehrer, (2002, September). Former WorldCom controller pleads guilty to fraud charges.
    Retrieved September 15, 2003, from http://www.pbs.org/newshour/updates/worldcom_09-26-
    02.html

Petry, E. (2002). Solid corporate ethics can be good business, too.
    Retrieved September 15, 2003 from http://www.helleniccomserve.com

Stone, A. (2002, June). MBA schools extend ethics emphasis. Retrieved September 15, 2003 from http://
    www.bizjournals.com/twincities/stories/2002/06/17/focus2.html?t=printable

CHAPTER

SIX

Managing Human Resources –

The Importance of Employee

Retention

Managing your company's greatest asset, its Human Resources, can be quite complicated at times. Many companies hire employees based simply on the need for a warm body, which is never a good idea. In addition, if a company finds itself in the headlines because of its troubles, those who are watching the situation the closest are the top employees. Those employees may decide it is time to go elsewhere. This makes the task of hiring and retaining quality employees even more challenging. This chapter explores the idea of hiring and retaining quality employees both in and out of crisis situations.

At times, there are companies that find themselves in trouble and in the headlines, but they are not ready to close their doors for good. If your company runs into difficult times, how would you get your top employees to stay? Are your top employees already leaving and do you know why? Have you ever heard of a retention strategy and do you have one? These are some questions to ask about your company while reading this chapter.

Introduction

When a company is in a period of financial crisis, how does it keep employees from bailing out and seeking employment elsewhere? The late 1990s and early 2000s have seen many companies in financial crisis, such as MCI WorldCom, USAir, and Kmart. Kmart filed for Chapter 11 bankruptcy, closed hundreds of stores, and laid off thousands of employees, but has now successfully emerged from bankruptcy. What did Kmart do to keep the core employees it needed to achieve this success?

Many companies talk about the importance of employee retention, but a recent statistic suggests that talk is all some companies are doing. According to Branham (2001, p. 3), "While 75 percent of senior executives say that employee retention is a major concern, only 15 percent have made it a strategic priority in their companies." In today's economy of low unemployment, it is becoming easier for employees to consider leaving a job to move to another. If a concerted effort is not made to retain employees, a business faces the daunting and expensive task of continually hiring and training new employees.

This chapter will discuss the importance of employee retention, the need for a retention strategy, and the importance of implementing the strategy, not only to keep the employees who work for your company, but also to be sure the retention strategies are in place if the company slips into a financial crisis. This chapter will also discuss examples of employee retention strategies gone right and wrong. Already having a retention strategy in place will certainly be a step in the right direction in keeping employees through a firm's difficult times.

Employee Retention – Why is it Important?

The importance of employee retention is an issue of money. Losing good employees can be costly to any business. First of all, it is going to cost the company money to hire a new employee to replace the one that has left. Secondly, losing good employees can be detrimental to the business if the customer-base is loyal to the employee rather than the company. Michaud (2002) writes, "According to the U.S. Department of Labor, it costs a company one-third of a new hire's annual salary to replace an employee. Using a modest annual salary of $35,000, a company can easily spend $11,550 for each new employee hired."

It is important to note that even the best retention strategy is not going to prevent turnover and there is nothing wrong with that. Some employees may leave to move to another community, some may decide to return to school, and some may retire. It is important to have some turnover in the organization because hiring new people also offers the opportunity for fresh ideas and new perspectives from the new employee. Additionally, if no one ever leaves the company, the employees are all going to be at the top of their salary range and payroll expense is going to be high.

If retaining employees is important, but it is a given that employees are going to leave, what is a manager to do in this seemingly catch-22 situation? Simply put, the focus should be on retaining the employees who are most vital to the organization. In an effort to determine what employees are the most vital; Branham (2001, p. 16-17) has created four groupings into which all employees of a company can be categorized. The groups are:

a. Star Performers (the top 10%),
b. High Performers (20-30%),
c. Steady Performers, and
d. Poor/Marginal Performers.

Knowing these four groups, Branham (2001, p.117) discusses selective retention, which is defined as "a process to be used by management to minimize the loss of those in the first three groups and to move those in the last group into other jobs where they can be more successful."

The concept of selective retention is important in creating a retention strategy. Note too, that Branham's definition focused on helping those in the last group find success, rather than terminating them. If possible, it is important to retain employees because it is less costly than hiring new ones. This does not mean that some poor performers may have to be terminated, but quite frequently it is possible to move an employee to another job or get them additional training.

Training is a critical element in employee retention. The type of training that employees crave and that is needed for competitive advantage today goes beyond that of what is needed to simply do the job. Training needs to start at an orientation, with a focus on continual on-the-job training throughout the employee's career with the company. As Adam Smith wrote so long ago, the person who constantly performs "a very few simple operations…generally becomes as stupid and ignorant as it is possible for a human creature to become" (qtd. in Levine, 1995, p. 36). Now, more than ever, companies need to employ the whole person and not just their hands.

Often an employee may take a job that is not a good fit, just for the sake of having a paycheck. So too, sometimes an employer will hire someone who is not a good fit for the sake of having a warm body. Either of these situations can lead an employee to the fourth group.

Why do Employees Leave?

As discussed in the previous section of this chapter, it is impossible (and not even desirable) to achieve a zero turnover rate among employees. Aside from those inevitable losses though, why do good employees leave a company? In order to develop a viable retention strategy, it is important to evaluate the reasons employees leave. In their book "Embracing Excellence," Ashby and Pell (2001, p. 3-12) show the results of a survey conducted among mid-level managers, asking them their complaints about their company's upper management. The survey results should provide sound insight into the reasons good employees leave organizations.

The first complaint (Ashby & Pell, 2001) mid-level managers have about upper-level management is inequity in pay. This was not a complaint about mid-level managers being paid inequitable amounts, but rather a complaint about upper-level managers receiving extravagant compensation packages. Offering CEOs and other high-level executives such packages is a generally accepted practice, but can become a very bitter pill for employees to swallow, especially in times of crisis, as will be illustrated later in this chapter.

The second complaint (Ashby & Pell, 2001) is a fear-based management style. This complaint encompasses things like constantly checking up on employees or not being tolerant when an employee disagrees with a manager. When managers manage by intimidation, their employees are not going to be comfortable in that working environment.

Lack of a clear career path is the third complaint (Ashby & Pell, 2001). When employees envision themselves staying with a company for an extended number of years, they want to know they have an opportunity to advance in their career. Many companies do not do a good enough job of making career paths visible to employees. This may be intentional, such as a family business where promotions generally go to family members, or it may just not occur to upper-management to make career paths clear to all employees.

The fourth complaint (Ashby & Pell, 2001) is tolerance of poor performance. There is no quicker way to destroy employee morale than to let poor performers continue employment. The employees who excel at their job can feel demoralized when they see an employee doing poorly and keeping their job. Morale continues to decrease as those poor performers are given similar compensation raises as the above-average employees.

Complaint number five (Ashby & Pell, 2001) is broken promises. People learn at an early age the importance of not breaking promises, yet it surfaces here as a complaint about upper-level managers. It bears repeating that managers need to keep promises. Failure to do so will result in employees who disbelieve anything the manager says.

The sixth complaint (Ashby & Pell, 2001) is putting personal interests ahead of what is best for the company. It is wrong for a manager to make a decision based on personal motivation, no matter the case. When a manager makes such a decision, it will create animosity among the employees.

Being treated as second-class citizens is the seventh complaint (Ashby & Pell, 2001). This corresponds with the fifth complaint (broken promises) in that it is the type of behavior one should learn at an early age to avoid. Still, many of the survey respondents indicated dissatisfaction with a superior who acted as if s/he were better than the employees s/he supervised.

Lack of reward for superior work is the eighth complaint (Ashby & Pell, 2001). This complaint could be related to the complaint about tolerance of poor performance. Employees who are not recognized for superior performance will eventually not strive so hard and settle into the status quo.

The final complaint is feeling unappreciated (Ashby & Pell, 2001). This complaint could be viewed as related to earlier ones. Like in other aspects of society, it is sometimes easy to be caught up in focusing on what is wrong and failing to recognize what is being done right. Managers can be caught up in this and it is crucial they work to avoid this pitfall.

As stated at the beginning of this section, these nine complaints provide valuable insight into the factors that cause employees to seek other employment. As a manager, it is a good idea to review this list and do a self-check.

How to Get Employees to Stay

Now that the reasons for employees leaving a company have been discussed, it is important to discuss what can be done to get employees to stay. The simple answer is to study the nine complaints in the previous section and take actions to correct any of those that exist in one's corporate culture. This section will incorporate the complaints from the previous discussion in detailing the motivations for employees to stay.

Michaud (2002) details five tips to maximum employee retention. The first tip is to build a strong relationship with every employee. Although it is a business relationship between manager and employee, it is important for the manager to "connect" with his/her employees. This is not to suggest that the manager be "best friends" with each of his/her employees. Nevertheless, the manager needs to strive to find something in common with each employee. Doing so will increase the perception among employees that they are important and appreciated. Without solid relationships, a manager should not expect to have his employees' full respect and loyalty.

Respect and loyalty are both very important keys to successful employee retention. A good example of this is the small information technology firm OMIX. Dr. Lillie, the Chief Operations Officer (COO) of OMIX believed "that a company could fulfill its practical needs while respecting employees' human needs" (TechRepublic, February 19, 2001). This corporate attitude had demonstrated success with:

> A turnover rate of less than 5 percent. Employees who deferred their salaries for months at times to ensure the company stayed afloat. Employees who worked long hours when necessary, without complaint. Employees who declined offers of more money and stock options from competitors. (TechRepublic, February 19, 2001)

Dr. Lillie, along with her co-founder husband, have a philosophy that manifested itself in many ways, but the most pervasive is simply that they take the employee's well being into consideration before their own wants and needs. The company once turned down a project because it would have taken up too much employee investment.

Michaud's (2002) second tip is to freely offer praise. As seen in the previous section, employees want to feel appreciated by their employer. A simple statement of "Good job!" or "Thanks for your help!" is a great way to show your employees you appreciate them. It is also a good idea to praise employees in public settings. The caveat is not to praise just for the sake of praising. If employees feel like the praise is hollow, it is not going to be effective. A manager committed to retaining valuable employees will be willing to dispense praise as deserved.

The third tip Michaud discusses is to truly listen to employee feedback. Michaud (2002) states, "Your employees will gladly tell you their needs and job-related issues. You simply need to listen to what they say and not dismiss their thoughts as wishful thinking or unimportant." An effective manager will listen closely to his/her employees and respond to their needs in the best manner possible.

Michaud's (2002) fourth tip is to keep the mood light. It is natural for people to enjoy having a good time and there is no reason work should not to be fun. Of course, it is important to keep the fun in check to not interfere with work. People who are smiling and laughing are going to enjoy their workplace. Studies have shown that fun and humor help alleviate stress, and an effective manager will figure out how to increase the level of fun while maintaining a healthy level of productivity.

The final tip in Michaud's (2002) article is for the manager to continually strengthen his/her team. This tip has a direct relationship to successful employee retention in that it is important when hiring a new employee to make sure the effort is expended to hire the right person for the job. As Michaud (2002) states, "If you initially hire second-rate candidates, you can expect high turnover. However, when you strive to hire those people whose strengths are your weaknesses, the entire company benefits."

What Happens When a Firm is in Crisis?

Knowing the reasons employees are likely to leave a firm and knowing what should be done to keep them from leaving, what happens when a firm finds itself in the midst of a financial crisis? One of the primary concerns in this situation is retaining the personnel the firm will need in order to successfully emerge from the crisis. If a firm files for Chapter 11 bankruptcy protection, consider what the employees are likely to do. It is a strong possibility that résumés are being updated, recruiters are being called, and newspaper want ads are being scanned. The company's future is dimmer than it used to be and the employees may start looking for jobs elsewhere. Not only that, but the company's competition may start attempting to recruit personnel away from the company in crisis. All of these situations are a blow to any company struggling to survive a crisis without the personnel in place.

Retaining employees in a crisis is a significant challenge. Not only has the company publicly announced (as in the case of a Chapter 11 bankruptcy) the problems it is facing, but the company must take steps towards resolving those problems. In the case of a financial crisis, many companies find themselves faced with difficult choices, such as "cutting staff, cutting benefits, changing work rules, or a combination of such actions" (Grossman, 2003).

In an attempt to retain the key personnel a firm identifies as necessary to emerge from crisis, many companies are utilizing retention bonuses, also sometimes called stay bonuses. As Bates (2003) states, "If there is an employee you really need because of his talent or knowledge, you pledge to pay him, for example, a certain amount over a period of time to entice him to stay." By this definition, retention bonuses are not limited to times of crisis. Bates gives an example of retention bonuses being used in high-tech industries where there is high demand for talented individuals. Firms offer retention bonuses to their employees to keep them from leaving for another firm. Not only is it an incentive to an employee to stay, it makes it more expensive for competitors to lure them away. As Bates (2003) says, "Offering retention bonuses 'won't make it expensive for somebody to steal one person, but it will make it expensive for a business to steal a lot of people. It protects you from being raided.'"

Recent headlines, however, have focused on the use of retention bonuses in times of crisis. Kmart is a company that successfully used retention bonuses when it filed for Chapter 11 bankruptcy. "According to documents filed in Kmart's bankruptcy, as of Jan. 1, 7,841 employees are in line for bonuses. Among them: vice-presidents, regional managers, 1,745 store managers, and 2,710 pharmacists and pharmacy managers" (Dixon, 2003). The combined total of the retention bonuses is estimated at $150 million. The retention bonuses were paid in installments; employees received fractions of the bonus as Kmart proceeded to emerge from Chapter 11. The balance was paid once the emergence was successful. Dixon's (2003) article also mentions, "U.S. Bankruptcy Court Judge Susan Pierson Sonderby allowed Kmart to set up its key employee retention plan in March 2002." This draws attention to the fact that a company filing for Chapter 11 can and must present to the court a plan for key employee retention (Bates, 2003).

The court wants a detailed strategy on the company's plan to keep the personnel required to keep the company going.

Another company that has received a lot of publicity in recent months for retention bonuses is AMR Corp.'s American Airlines. On April 15, 2003, AMR's three unions were voting on whether to accept cuts in employee compensation in benefits, in an effort to help save the endangered airline. That same day, AMR filed its annual report with the Securities and Exchange Commission, in which plans for retention bonuses were revealed. In particular, the AMR board had called for the:

> Creation of a trust to protect supplemental pension benefits for 45 senior American executives. In addition, the board last year offered 'retention bonuses' – equal to twice base salary – to American's top six executives if they stay with the troubled airline through January 2005. (McCartney, April 17, 2003)

The plans for these extravagant bonuses had never been revealed to employees, who were upset to learn of them at the same time they were contemplating pay cuts between 15.6% and 23% (McCartney, April 17, 2003).

The core problem in this instance is that AMR CEO, Mr. Donald F. Carty, chose not to publicize the planned retention bonuses, for fear that "American's benefits would appear modest compared with those granted at other carriers" (McCartney, April 22, 2003). Subsequent to this decision, Mr. Carty resigned as AMR CEO (McCartney, April 25, 2003) and American's top executives agreed to forego their retention bonuses (though they opted to keep the supplemental pension trust). In the wake of Mr. Carty's departure, AMR successfully negotiated with its three unions to concessions that would allow AMR to avoid filing for Chapter 11 protection. Part of the negotiations included "Potential bonuses up to 10% for employees" ("AMR Flight Attendants", 2003).

The problems AMR faced have a direct relation to the employee complaints detailed earlier in this chapter. Deciding to keep the existence of the retention bonuses from the company's employees certainly caused feelings of hurt, anger, and mistrust. Management must always be sensitive to its employees and treat them with respect. It is a good idea to always remember the Golden Rule.

Conclusion

This chapter has discussed the importance of employee retention. Most importantly, employee retention needs more than just lip service by management. Today's economy is an employee's market; low unemployment makes it easy for employees to switch jobs. Gone are the days of previous generations where people worked for the same company 25-30 years. Today's generation is accustomed to job-hopping and there are no signs of that changing. Branham (2001, p. 1) writes, "By the year 2008, there will be 161M jobs, but only 154M people to fill those jobs – a shortfall of 7 million. Employers must work hard to retain the talent they have."

There is no single "silver bullet" that will solve the problem of employee retention. Retention begins with the hiring process, making sure that the right person is hired for the right job. Retention efforts must continue throughout the employee's tenure with the company. Doing these things will put companies in a better position to retain employees in the event of a financial crisis. As the discussion of AMR shows, it is also important at all times, but especially during a crisis, that management not try to deceive or keep information from its employees. If a company is truly going to emerge from a crisis, it will do so because of the efforts of all its employees.

References

AMR flight attendants accept pay concessions. (2003, April 25). Retrieved April 25, 2003, from http://www.wsj.com

Ashby, F. & Pell, A. (2001). *Embracing excellence.* Paramus, NJ: Prentice Hall Press.

Bates, S. (2003, May). Staying power. *HR Magazine, 48,* 67-75.

Branham, L. (2001). *Keeping the people who keep you in business.* New York: American Management Association.

Dixon, J. (2003, April 9). Kmart giving out bonuses to many loyalists. Retrieved April 9, 2003, from http://www.freep.com/money/business/bonus9_20030409.htm

Grossman, R. (2003, May). Holding back bankruptcy. *HR Magazine, 48,* 45-52.

Levine, D. (1995). *Reinventing the workplace: how business and employees can both win.* Washington, D.C: The Brookings Institution.

McCartney, S. (2003, April 17). AMR unions express fury over management benefits. Retrieved April 17, 2003, from http://www.wsj.com.

McCartney, S. (2003, April 22). AMR's decision to keep quiet about perks could undo pacts. Retrieved April 22, 2003, from http://www.wsj.com

McCartney, S. (2003, April 25). Carty steps down as AMR chief amid fallout over executive perks. Retrieved April 25, 2003, from http://www.wsj.com

Michaud, L. (2002). Turn the tables on employee turnover: five keys to maximum employee retention. Retrieved March 26, 2003, from http://www.frogpond.com/printversion.cfm?articleid=lmichaud02

TechRepublic. (February 19, 2001). IT company's unique management style leads to happier employees and higher profits. Retrieved from http://www.omix.com/html12.news.coverages/tr.html

CHAPTER

SEVEN

Critical Issues In Leadership

What makes a leader and how do leaders differ from managers? All problems faced by any company are caused by a lack of leadership in some area. Thus, leadership is essential to the survival and growth of all organizations. This chapter will explore the traits that leaders possess and why it is so important to maintain good leadership. It relies intensively on Oren Harari's description of Colin Powell to explain what qualities true leaders possess.

Some of the companies already mentioned throughout this book are found here again in order to illustrate the failures in leadership within those companies. It is our hope that you will find many of the good traits mentioned within your own leadership team and very few of the bad traits.

Introduction

Leadership is a key to any successful organization. With the right people in place, a company can be very prosperous. If the wrong people are in leadership positions, the company may not survive for long. When companies begin to fail, it is usually found that the leadership hired by the Board of Directors has fallen short of expectations.

This chapter will discuss the qualities that are necessary for successful leadership. It will also provide examples of companies that have suffered serious crises because of poor leadership within their organizations.

Description of Leadership

Colin Powell describes leadership as, "the art of accomplishing more than the science of management says is possible" (Harari, 2002, p. 13). From this definition, it can be seen that leadership and management are two different things. Although great leaders and great managers share some qualities, it still takes a great leadership team to make things happen. It also takes a leader at the top to make the tough decisions. Stephen R. Covey defines the role of leadership as, "deal[ing] with direction, leadership deals with vision" (Covey, 1990,
p. 246).

Sometimes it takes making people angry to get the job done. Leaders will not be liked all of the time. Treating everyone in the same manner, fair and equal, only causes the top producers to let up on their work. When this happens, creativity ceases and the downward spiral toward failure begins, because the top producers view their efforts as no more important than those who produce poorly. A leader must treat people according to their efforts and reward them in that fashion. When others see the rewards that good efforts receive, their own quality of work starts to improve.

The day problems are not discussed openly within an organization is the day that leadership has failed. The perception is that most CEOs think they are well above the people that work for them. This will close a line of communication that is crucial to the leadership in keeping them informed about how the company is running. If the employees feel that leaders do not care for them, how can a leader expect them to care about the company? As Covey (1990, p. 109) says, "At the root of most communication problems are perception or credibility problems."

A leader esteeming themselves too highly happens all too often. As they move up, leaders may tend to forget from where they came. Once they become the 'expert,' leaders sometimes implement ideas that are just not going to work. When this happens, they have become detached from the real world.

Sometimes the pros need to be challenged. Even the pros can level out. They may have reached their current maximum capabilities. When this happens, leadership has created a 'yes' man. This kind of person has become lazy in the company. By challenging the pros, leadership is keeping them aggressive and productive.

Another lesson leaders can learn from Colin Powell is to never neglect the details. As people move up through management, the thought comes to mind to delegate some of the tasks that are assigned. This comes from having an increased workload as progression is made through the company. This is a good idea, but as they move up, good leaders still know to pay attention to the details. They follow through with the directions given and look around to make sure something is not forgotten. One small, forgotten detail can cause a person or an organization to fail.

As a leader, one should not seek specific permission for every little project. If one looks hard enough, someone can always be found to reject a good idea. Obviously, some discretion needs to be used, but good leaders believe that if they have not been told 'no,' they can go ahead and do it. If the leader makes a mistake and the idea does not work out as expected, then s/he learns not to do it again. Jim Rohn (1991, p. 23) states, "One way to learn to do something right is to do something wrong. We learn from our failures as well as successes."

Companies and their leaders have to keep looking deep. The attitude that 'everything is going fine, why change it' can cause failures to be overlooked and is when things can start to fall apart. Why would a leader want to invest in a new idea when no one likes to change? Good leaders always look for ways to change things for the better.

All too often, leaders forget how they made it to their current position in the company. It is the employees around them that help leaders achieve top-level management positions. Only when leaders have surrounded themselves with quality individuals do they achieve their leadership goals.

Giving people titles and placing them on a chart of succession does not really mean anything. Anyone can be given a title, but employees know who the real leaders are. Individuals who have been given titles might achieve minimal results, but they will not truly be 'the leader' until they take the reins and develop a vision and provide direction.

Great leaders do not let their egos get in the way. If leaders do not think of self-improvement, others will, and they will be plotting to take over the leadership positions. In a fast paced economy, individuals can become obsolete before they know it. Leaders need to continually improve their skills and make the changes necessary to enhance their position within their organizations. When making changes, leaders must also make sure that the old ways are removed so that one can continue forward. Stephen R. Covey (1990, p. 281) uses the term 'transformational leadership' for those who go and learn the new ways to do things on a daily basis.

Many companies fall into the trap of chasing the latest management fads. Fads are just that, something that comes and goes very quickly. If leaders stick to their core values but remain flexible, they are better able to change as each situation requires. By following fads and changing their leadership styles every time a new one emerges, leaders lose a lot of credibility among their employees.

Optimism means seeing the glass half full instead of half empty. It means leaders that have the vision they will be able to accomplish any task set in front of them. Complaining all the time when changes occur only doubles the work effort needed to accomplish tasks. Some leaders continually fight change and blame those around them when things do not go as planned. Optimism allows leaders to see that there are ways to achieve the goals set forth. It gives hope that they are going to succeed.

Choosing the right people to surround the leaders of an organization has become more difficult than ever. Most of the time when an individual is hired, the trend is to look at past accomplishments. What someone has done in the past is not always an indicator as to what that person can do now or in the future. Great leaders surround themselves with those who have integrity, loyalty, high energy, and the drive to accomplish the goals of the company. Leaders should hire those who are skilled and knowledgeable in their individual areas, because this can make up for the things that a leader may lack.

Keeping communications and actions as simple as possible provides the ability for everyone to understand what is expected of them. Leaders should break down their visions and long-term plans so that all employees can understand them. No one can plan for everything and no one can see the plan as the leaders do. Good leaders keep everyone informed of any changes that may occur. By keeping things simple, it is easier for everyone to react to changes.

All too often, leaders wait until they have every single fact available to them before they take action. In Colin Powell's formula, "P = 40 to 70, P stands for probability of success" (Harari, 2002, p. 260). If a leader waits for all the facts to come in, someone else may take action and get the job done first. Sometimes leaders are afraid of taking risks. This fear could stem from earlier failures that have not been forgotten. However, fear of taking risk can actually be a greater risk to an organization and can increase the chance for failure.

Great leaders listen to the management on the production lines. They are the ones who are making the money that the company brings in. These managers realize very quickly when something is not working. Successful leaders listen to that advice and make changes that will help. Good leaders visit with their employees periodically and really listen to them. Staying behind closed doors and analyzing data does not always give leaders a good feel of what is actually happening within their organizations.

Many leaders are caught up in all that is happening around them and forget to take a break once the task is complete. Taking time off when a job is finished is not a sin. Some leaders believe that to stay on top they have to constantly keep working. This leads to stress related ailments and burnout. Leaders need a vacation to relax and rejuvenate themselves. Some leaders view wealth as happiness; actually wealth is an effect of happiness (Rohn, 1991, p. 100).

Ultimately, the final responsibility for the success or failure of an organization belongs to the leaders. No matter how an organization is set up, the individuals at the top own the failures and successes of a company. Some shirk this responsibility and try to pass it off onto someone else. This is why it can be a lonely position at the top. No matter how open an organization is, true leaders will find that they are alone more often than not.

Failed Leadership – Kmart

Kmart is one company that found out the hard way that its new leadership was not what everyone thought it was. The department store chain's woes started approximately ten years ago. At that time, Wal-Mart took over the top spot as the number one retailer in the country. Kmart embarked on a rejuvenation plan to keep up with Wal-Mart.

During this time period, Floyd Hall retired as the CEO of Kmart, and Chuck Conway was brought in from the CVS store chain. Kmart acquired Chief Operations Officer (COO) Mark Schwartz, who was a Wal-Mart veteran, to help provide insight on how to catch Wal-Mart.

Conway had a two-year plan to revitalize Kmart. This plan included spending $1.8 billion on new technology (Howell, March 2002, para. 2 & 3). Conway also set a plan into operation that would try to capitalize on every day low prices and the expansion into super stores. A lot of this sounds familiar because this is what Wal-Mart was doing. Conway is not totally to blame for Kmart's failure. He just happened to be in charge when the fallout started and he did bring Mark Schwartz on board.

Going back a little further into Kmart history, it can be seen some former leaders made mistakes. Growth stalled under the leadership of Joseph Antonini. Kmart had operational control of OfficeMax, Borders Books, Payless Drugs, and Builders Square. These acquisitions by Kmart took place when the company was at the top and had a positive cash flow. Some say it might have ventured into too many areas and could not control all the acquisitions. Because of this, Antonini was fired in January 1995, and by March 1995, was replaced by Floyd Hall (Howell, February 2002).

One problem that had been plaguing Kmart for quite some time was inventory that was consistently out of stock in the stores. When customers cannot find what they want, they will go elsewhere to find it. Leadership did not recognize this nor did it listen to its store managers. Kmart was trying to keep up with fads, instead of building on its core products and expanding that market.

Conway's hiring of Schwartz is one of the mistakes for which he took the blame. As described earlier, Schwartz came from Wal-Mart, and upon further investigation, it was found that he had previously been at the helm of some other failed companies. It is important that every company have its own identity. Differentiation between companies is the reason why customers patronize their establishments. Kmart had lost its identity by trying to look like Wal-Mart, and that is what caused Kmart's trouble.

Failed Leadership-Enron

Enron is one of the most publicized leadership failures in history. Many of its leaders were put into positions based on who they were instead of what they could do for the company. It was a deception that began as soon as deregulation of energy started. The company grew so quickly, the leaders thought they were untouchable. Greed also played a major role in the downfall of Enron. As soon as the leadership realized there were grave problems within the company, a cover-up began. Perhaps the leaders thought if they could change some laws and draw things out, it might provide some time to recover some money and allow them to correct their mistakes. As the company spun out of control, the leadership decided to take what it could and run. As top management left the company, those who took the vacated positions found that the downward spiral destroying Enron could not be stopped. In only eight short months, Enron collapsed after sixteen years in business. The ramifications of the fall of Enron are still being felt worldwide.

Both of these examples show how poor leadership can damage or destroy a company. With Kmart, it was the leadership's misjudgment of what the company could actually do that led to its decline. Instead of maintaining productivity in its core business and continuing to improve on what it had, the leaders acted as if no one could knock them out of the number one retail spot. Some Boards of Directors have positioned people in key places that have led companies into, and out of, bankruptcy. A leader's willingness to admit that things have not gone the way that was envisioned shows a strong commitment toward the company.

Enron, on the other hand, violated the one quality that is the hardest to earn back. The leaders did not guard their integrity. When the problems started, Enron leaders tried to cover them up or disguise them instead of figuring out how to solve them. The leaders created a false sense of security and overstated the facts to benefit themselves. This deception not only hurt Enron's reputation, but it ruined the lives of many innocent people. Many employees had been with the company from its beginning and had most of their financial stability invested in the company. The falsehoods generated by the Enron leadership were maintained up until the final financial collapse, when it was too late for the majority of employees to save themselves.

Conclusion

Leadership should never be taken lightly. Learning some basic principles of leadership provides for a successful business environment. It brings a positive atmosphere that provides for stability and growth in a company, which is advantageous to all concerned. Leadership plays one of the most important roles in making a company successful. With someone in place who has not learned the basic roles that a leader plays, any changes that the leader tries to implement to make improvements will not succeed. A leader is not a manager; s/he is an innovator, a role model, an influencer, and a mentor. A leader must have vision and be able to translate that vision into successful actions. When a leader does these things failure is not an option.

References

Covey, S. (1990). *Principle centered leadership*. New York: Fireside.

Harari, O. (2002). *The leadership secrets of Colin Powell*. New York: McGraw-Hill.

Howell, D. (2002, March 11). Kmart in crisis. *DSN Retailing Today*. Retrieved August 1, 2003, from http://www.findarticles.com/cf

Howell, D. (2002, Feb. 11). Kmart signs on new execs. *DSN Retailing Today*. Retrieved August 1, 2003, from http://www.findarticles.com/cf

Rohn, J. (1991). *The five major pieces to the life puzzle*. Southlake, Texas:

Jim Rohn International.

CHAPTER

EIGHT

The Value of Quality Management

There are many programs available today to help a company focus on achieving quality in products and services. The use of at least one quality program is essential for corporate competitive advantage. However, what is shown throughout this book and in recent history is that where corporations may be most sorely lacking in quality is within the leadership ranks. In the pages of this chapter, you will find both disturbing and uplifting facts about today's leaders of corporate America. This chapter will serve to remind us all that quality starts at the top. Quality leaders=Quality Employees=Quality Workplaces=Quality Products and Services.

Introduction

In the past, many companies have either ignored quality or not had the proper knowledge of the need to focus on it. This chapter will outline some of today's methods and programs for management to use in increasing the quality of their operations. To illustrate the need of management to also focus on quality leadership, examples will be given of companies that are letting their upper management have free reign with the company's fortunes, as well as those that are actually implementing "quality management practices" and/or adhering to globally recognized quality standards.

Quality Management Programs

Corporations are now turning toward more innovative methods to run their business. There has been a major trend toward getting executives through training such as Six Sigma Green and Black Belt training. "Six Sigma" is an integrated, disciplined, proven approach for improving measurable results for any organization. The training program provides business process improvement to include Total Quality Management (TQM) techniques that apply both up and down the workforce chain. It also provides a management improvement program that includes training, consulting, and support services. Lean Manufacturing (a new and innovative thought process and philosophy for the manufacturing industry) is also taught in the Six Sigma program.

One great thinker that influenced the ideas of Six Sigma was Walter Shewhart. A former Bell telephone employee, he is known as the grandfather of Total Quality Management. Shewhart "preached the importance of adapting management processes to create profitable situations for both businesses and consumers, promoting the utilization of his own creation -- the SPC control chart" (Skymark.com, 2003). Creating an output of information regarding a process, therefore allowing management to better manage a process is the intent of statistical process control.

Another method Shewhart utilized contains a cycle of four continuous steps: Plan, Do, Study, and Act. Shewhart believed that following these steps (commonly referred to as the PDSA cycle) would lead to total quality improvement (Skymark.com, 2003). "The cycle draws its structure from the notion that constant evaluation of management practices -- as well as the willingness of management to adopt and disregard unsupported ideas --are keys to the evolution of a successful enterprise" (Skymark.com 2003).

Another great thinker whose ideas influence quality management today is Dr. Juran, who was the first to incorporate the human aspect of quality management, or Total Quality Management. Juran tends to focus more on customer needs and identity to improve quality. The "Quality Control Handbook," first released in 1951, is still the standard reference work for quality managers and based on the following trilogy (SkyMark.com 2003):

Quality Trilogy:

Quality Planning	Identify who are the customers. Determine the needs of those customers. Translate those needs into our language. Develop a product that can respond to those needs. Optimize the product features so as to meet our needs and customer needs.
Quality Improvement	Develop a process which is able to produce the product. Optimize the process.
Quality Control	Prove that the process can produce the product under operating conditions with minimal inspection. Transfer the process to Operations.

Today, the Juran Institute is one of the leading quality management consultant firms in the world, and it produces books, workbooks, videos and other materials to support the wide use of Dr. Juran's methods. The institute and the consulting practice continue to thrive today. Dr. Juran worked to promote quality management into his 90s, and only recently retired from his semi-public life (Skymark.com 2003).

The human aspect of quality management also shows up in "The 7 Habits of Highly Effective People," a national bestseller by Dr. Stephen R. Covey. It has been a great tool for millions of people and corporations in helping them maintain a "healthy corporate environment." The Franklin Covey web site (http://www.franklincovey.com, 2003) states, "Quick-fix solutions do not work in this environment. Piecemeal improvements are futile. Only those organizations that have made the effort to build a solid foundation of highly effective people will move surely and safely toward their destinations." Dr. Covey's book has been converted into The Franklin Covey's 7 Habits Workshop, an incredibly motivating workshop for all who attend. The 7 Habits are: (1) Be Proactive, (2) Begin with the End in Mind, (3) Put First Things First, (4) Think Win-Win, (5) Seek First to Understand, Then to Be Understood, (6) Synergize, and (7) Sharpen the Saw. These habits or principles continually help renovate thousands of organizations throughout the world by transforming the people they depend on, changing their mindsets, bringing in a different way of thinking.

When discussing quality management, it is important to mention The Baldrige National Quality Program Award, better known as the Baldrige award. It is named for Malcolm Baldrige, who served as U.S. Secretary of Commerce from 1981 until death in 1987. The following is an excerpt from the National Institute of Standards and Technology (2003) web site:

> His managerial excellence contributed to long-term improvement in efficiency and effectiveness of government. Because the leadership of the United States in product and process quality has been challenged strongly (and sometimes successfully) by foreign competition, and our nation's productivity growth has improved less than our competitors' over the last two decades. American business and industry are beginning to understand that poor quality costs companies as much as 20 percent of sales revenues nationally and that improved quality of goods and services goes hand in hand with improved productivity, lower costs, and increased profitability. Strategic planning for quality and quality improvement programs, through a commitment to excellence in manufacturing and services, are becoming increasingly essential to the well being of our nation's economy and our ability to compete effectively in the global marketplace.

Established in 1988, the Baldrige award recognizes companies and/or corporations for the continuous improvements in the areas of business, health care, and education.

International Organization for Standardization (ISO) is a set of standards for quality management systems that is readily accepted around the world. These standards, developed and adopted in 1987, were revised in 1994 and again in 2000 to keep up with the ever-changing demands of the business world. According to ISO Easy (2003), "currently more than 90 countries have adopted ISO 9000 as national standards." The purchase of a product or service from an organization that is registered to the ISO 9000 standards assures the purchaser that the quality they receive is what they expect. The year 2000 revisions incorporated quality objectives, monitoring customer satisfaction, and continual improvement to provide the customer higher assurances that their expectations and needs are met. The ISO 9001 standard is intended for a quality management assessment system. With all this said, many companies now require that their suppliers be ISO 9001 certified, an avenue that ensures they can provide a quality finished product to their customers.

There are many programs to choose from, of which these are only a few. Although these programs are necessary for increasing the quality of a company's products or services, many companies now find themselves in crisis because they do not focus on quality within their management. The rest of this chapter will demonstrate the need for quality within management with examples of the quality of management within some companies.

Overcompensation, Disarray, and Corruption within the C.E.O. Ranks

The November, 2003 issue of "Quality Digest," contained an article that discussed how people felt about their job; it broke the survey down into many areas, but two that were very interesting were: how do you feel about your compensation with respect to your work responsibilities? Secondly, how do you feel about your boss and or management, as well as the company for which you work? It was notable to read that "the level of job satisfaction has been steadily on the decline since reaching nearly 59% in 1995" according to Lynn Franco, director of The Conference Board's Consumer Research Center. "As technology transforms the workplace, accelerating the pace of activities, increasing expectations and productivity demands, and blurring the lines between work and play-workers are steadily growing unhappy with their jobs." The job satisfaction figure has now decreased to 43.2%

The shift to fewer happy employees has become more apparent throughout the workforce. The Quality Digest article attributed many factors to this disgruntled feeling in the workforce. However, probably the most important factor is that bonus plans and salaries are starting to receive substantially poor ratings, as only 20% are satisfied with the plan/salaries their company has in place; those 20% being the individuals that are in upper management and\or sit on the Board of Directors.

According to McClayland (1999), the average CEO of a major corporation made 42 times the pay of a typical American factory worker in 1980. By 1990, that ratio had more than doubled 85 times and almost quintupled again to a staggering 419 times in 1998. If that rate of exponential growth continues, the average CEO will make the salary equivalent of more than 150,000 American factory workers in 2050. McClayland (1999), also states that, "the average salary and bonus for a chief executive rose a phenomenal 39%, to $2.3 million in 1996. Retirement benefits, incentive plans, and gains from stock options are also added to the CEO's compensation package." This type of increase in CEO pay is sending a disturbing message. Managers, supervisors, and other key employees responsible for day-to-day company activities are receiving much smaller compensation for their efforts.

How are the workers of today's workforce supposed to feel when they know that upper management is making many times the salary of the average worker? Does this trend inspire the average worker to produce at high quality levels? What sort of plans are in place for workers to want to achieve excellence in day-to-day performance of their duties when all they see in the headlines is that the CEO of XYZ Corporation just landed another golden parachute? To what types of standards are these CEOs being held? What we have witnessed in recent history is the debacle with Enron overstating assets and corporate executives pillaging the corporate funds, the fallout and demise of WorldCom, and the heavily tarnished reputation of Martha Stewart resulting from insider trading charges. It is obvious that quality in management needs to be re-established so that investor, consumer, and employee confidence can be restored.

There is no doubt that CEOs are making big bucks by being the person in charge. However, some are questioning whether the CEOs deserve all the money they are making. CEOs are expected to put a lot of time and effort into trying to make their company a success. There is one question left to answer: Is the CEO's time worth more than the factory worker who is standing on the assembly line making the company's product for a minimum wage?

According to the article "Start a Campaign to Curb Runaway CEO Pay" (2004), there are ways to fight runaway CEO pay. The first step you should take is to get inside the boardroom. Find out about the role that your company's Board of Directors and Compensation Committee play in approving salaries. Another way to fight excessive compensation is to use your shareholder influence. If you own shares of stock, use your shareholder power to oppose excessive CEO salaries. A third thing you can do is to rally your co-workers and community. When it comes to excessive CEO pay and corporate practices that threaten jobs, no one has more at stake than the workers and their communities. This web site also lists alerting the IRS, contacting the SEC, and participating in campaigns as ways to fight runaway CEO compensation.

These high-ranking individuals are obviously very happy with the bonus packages and salaries they receive. For example, Michael Eisner of Disney, made $737 million during the last five years. That's about

19 times the $38 million made by the average CEO on Forbes.com's First Annual CEO Value Survey. While Eisner's personal income grew during that time, Disney's five-year net income shrank an average of 3.1% yearly. The average company included in the survey grew its net income by 19% over the five-year period. Michael Eisner has not always been perceived as an overpaid executive. Coming from Paramount Pictures in 1984, he was hired to give struggling Disney a jump-start. Not only did he do that, he turned the company into a media powerhouse. Under Eisner's management, Disney acquired ABC in 1995. Disney also grew its market capitalization from less than $2 billion back in 1984 to about $61 billion today. (Schiffman, 2003).

However, Eisner's reign as the leader of Disney has not been without criticism, and his compensation has long been a bone of contention with stockholders. Now, Eisner has the reputation of a guy that "can't play well with others." After his right-hand man, Disney President Frank Wells, died in a helicopter crash in 1994, Eisner went through several high-profile executives. According to Schiffman (2003), former Disney studio head Jeffrey Katzenberg (now of DreamWorks) sued the company for what he claimed was owed him as part of his contractual agreement; Disney finally settled for a reported $250 million. In an equally unfortunate decision, Eisner hired his longtime friend and Hollywood power broker Michael Ovitz to replace Wells. Ovitz lasted in the position for about one year and ended up costing Disney roughly $90 million in severance. It seems as if Eisner has not been exercising sound business practices as of late, in fact relationships within the Disney Board of Directors has led to the resignation of Roy Disney Jr.

Matthew Herper writes in an article at *Forbes.com* (2003) a story entitled "Hero's or Zeros? Best Value Bosses," which discusses compensation for 278 corporations. In this article, Herper points out some of the worst performing CEOs. Of them, Joseph Pichler of supermarket chain Kroger and Robert Peterson of meat-packer IP took home millions of dollars while their companies shrank by Forbes measures. Another poor performer was America Online's CEO, Steve Case. He earned $33.5 million over three years, while the return on equity was a negative 413 percent (McClayland, 1999). There is much talk about when AOL will split off from its Time Warner combined stock and become its own entity. Now apparently the split will happen after a $45 billion loss reported in early 2003 and over $100 billion in write-downs for 2002-2003, according to an article in the *International Herald Tribune* (O'Brien, 2003).

In the December 15, 2003 issue of Business Week, the cover story "Boeing, What Really Happened," discusses Boeing's $18 billion dollar contract for the Pentagon that is now being put on hold. Amidst allegations of "wrongdoings" by CFO Michael Sears, for hiring practice violations, chairman and chief executive Phil Condit resigned. The article states that starting with founder William Boeing:

> The company has been led by a succession of strong, commanding leaders who enjoyed near total autonomy, and led modest lives…Condit may have enjoyed a similar degree of latitude, but was further removed from the company's operations. He also developed a reputation as a womanizer, often with Boeing employees, and had an appetite for the high life. In a hiatus between one of his four marriages, Condit took up residence in the Boeing suite at Seattle's Four Seasons Olympic Hotel, where he had the suite remodeled at company expense into a private bedroom. (Holmes, 2003)

Condit's troubles began almost as soon as he took over as CEO; within a year he led the company into a manufacturing crisis that shook up Wall Street and caused the company to take a $2.6 billion write-off. Amidst accusations by shareholders of company deceit in accounting practices, Boeing paid $92 million to the shareholders after the merger with McDonnell Douglas. Through most of Condit's tenure, he completely misread the rising threat from Europe's Airbus, which some say could be the demise of the corporation's foothold in the aircraft-manufacturing sector. Some analysts also say that the acquisitions Condit made to diversify the corporation away from commercial aircraft were plagued with integration problems, leading Boeing to take more than $1 billion in write offs for this year alone. (Holmes, 2003) Where was the quality in the financial planning of all these mergers and acquisitions? Where was the leadership to properly integrate these new corporations under Boeing's corporate umbrella?

Corporations Going in the Right Direction

The December 15, 2003 issue of Business Week contained an interesting quote that says, "If this were your company, would you really spend your money this way?" The quote was from Bill Ford, CEO of Ford Motor Co., in regards to a new cost-conscious "mindset" he would like to instill in employees. Ford has seen his own company go through its share of problems, but through following the teaching of Deming, he believes his company is right on track.

William Clay Ford Jr. says he never planned to run the company his great-grandfather founded a century ago. Even now, two years after he fired former CEO Jacques A. Nasser, Ford insists he would have preferred to remain chairman of the $162 billion Ford Motor Co., according to a *Business Week Online* article entitled "Bill Ford's Long, Hard Road" (Kerwin, 2002). "I never really did fight for this job," Ford insisted, saying he took it out of "a sense of responsibility." While under Nasser's control, Ford had fallen into a miserable state of disrepair: Its profits, market share, quality, and morale were all spiraling downward as he tried to turn Ford it into something, anything, other than a traditional car company. Then there was the disastrous recall of Firestone tires, which damaged the company's image and cost $3.5 billion. By late October 2001, Ford decided he had to take charge. He acknowledges that the board could have acted more quickly in mid-2001, but says it was lulled by the record $7.2 billion profits of 1999. "It wasn't a gradual decline," he says. "It was a massive implosion." The company lost $5.5 billion in 2002, and barely broke even in 2003. Bill Ford has put his family name and fortune on the line; with an ever-watchful eye, he feels the company will succeed (Kerwin, 2002).

Back in the 1980s, it took the introduction of Taurus, plus cutting billions in expenses, for the company to eventually recover. Bill Ford's five-year turnaround plan could put the automaker solidly back in the black. His plan includes reducing costs by $4.5 billion, closing a maximum of six plants, and continuing to replace the out-of-date mass-volume cars such as Taurus with vehicles geared to more specific consumer tastes. Ford does have a few promising vehicles including the overhauled F-150 pickup, Ford's top-selling vehicle. In 2004, the automaker is launching two pivotal vehicles: the Ford Five Hundred big sedan and the CrossTrainer, a car-SUV hybrid, both of which have received mixed early reviews. In the late 1990s, Ford could not help but pull in the money. In North America, it made an average of $1,955 for each vehicle it sold. But by mid-2002, Ford was losing $190 per vehicle because of bloated costs and intense pricing pressure from General Motors Corp., a far more efficient manufacturer (Kerwin, 2002).

Ford has "shored up" the failing company exceedingly well. In 2003, Ford Motor Company moved up two spots from dead last among the seven major automakers in the benchmark J.D. Power & Associates initial quality survey (a major voice in the manufacturing industry). According to Ford:

> The new vehicle launches have been on schedule, and there have been no major recalls… Warranty claims are down about 10%, quarterly profits have exceeded analysts' forecasts, and the company's cash level is up to $9.4 billion--in part because Bill Ford took to the road in late January to promote a convertible preferred offering that ultimately raised $4.5 billion. (Kerwin, 2002)

A major factor in the equation is that Bill Ford brings to his family's company a consistency of purpose it has been missing through a series of short-run CEOs eager to hastily put their own brand on the automaker. "Bill is here for the long run," says Chief Financial Officer Allan D. Gilmour, according to Kerwin's article (2002). If so, the article states, he stands a chance of avoiding what he calls Detroit's "collective amnesia," an unerring knack for repeating the same mistakes: letting quality slip, ignoring changing consumer tastes, allowing costs to balloon, and making unwise acquisitions. During the next auto boom, "cash will be king," Ford promises. "It's burned in my brain. It's a matter of keeping our focus when things start to go well."

A related article by McClayland (1999) names two CEOs, Bill Gates of Microsoft and James Preston of Avon Products, as the best-performing executives over a three-year period. According to the article, Gates made $1.436 million in total pay from 1994 to 1996. He gave Microsoft shareholders a very good return for their investment. Microsoft's shareholders received a 310 percent return for the period.

Likewise, Preston, whose three-year total pay was $7.907 million, accumulated the highest return on equity. Relative to Preston's pay, Avon's return on equity was 141 percent for the three-year average. Another example is Warren Buffett, who during 2001 earned a total of $500,000. His company, Berkshire Hathaway, had a five-year total growth rate of 26%. Translated, that means he provided one percentage point of growth for just $19,000 (Herper, 2001).

Conclusion

This chapter has given some useful information on quality programs that can be implemented to pull a company out of crisis. However, quality in management is always necessary and, as has been shown in the examples, can make or break a company. This chapter also covered some issues that affect the way a workforce reacts to their workplace when bad management is in place. There will always be disparities in pay and compensation within the "ranks," however it us up to managers, supervisors, and board members to recognize these issues and address them in a timely manner. It is also wise for any corporation to avoid 'letting the fox watch the henhouse.'

There are many companies bordering on the brink of disaster, and their boards of directors must act quickly to prevent any further damage from happening. There were those companies that did not recognize in time that they were headed in a downward spiral, or maybe that their executives were taking what they wanted and leaving the company in complete disarray. However, as also mentioned in this chapter, there are companies such as Avon Products, Ford, and Microsoft that are preparing for the future. Companies can either ignore the need for quality in products/services as well as in management, or they can embrace the need and implement changes. If your business or corporation were on the brink of bankruptcy or collapse, which direction would you take?

References

Covey, F. (2003). The 7 habits of highly effective people. Retrieved January 24, 2004, from http://www. franklincovey.com.

Herper, M. (2001). Heroes or zeros? Best value bosses. Retrieved December 8, 2003, from http://www. forbes.com/2001/04/26/ceoindex.html

Holmes, S. (2003, December 15). Boeing, what really happened? *Business Week*, 32+.

Kerwin, K. (2002). Bill Ford's long, hard road. *BusinessWeek Online*. Retrieved December 8, 2003, from http://www.businessweek.com/magazine/content/02_40/b3802091.htm

ISO Easy. (2003). Welcome to ISO easy. Retrieved January 24, 2004, from http://www.isoeasy.org/.

McClayland, S. (1999). CEO compensation. Retrieved December 7, 2003, from http://academic.emporia.edu/smithwil/s99mg444/eja/mcclay.htm.

National Institute of Standards and Technology. (2003). Baldrige National Quality Program. Retrieved December 5, 2003, from http://www.quality.nist.gov/Improvement_Act.htm

O'Brien, T. (2003). Wall Street wonders if AOL can right itself. Retrieved January 26, 2004, from http://www.iht.com/articles/85187.html

Quality Digest. (2003, November). Job satisfaction at record low. Retrieved December 9, 2003, from http://www.qualitydigest.com/nov03/news.shtml#1

'Schiffman', B. (2001). Michael Eisner: mouse in a gilded mansion. *Forbes Magazine*. Retrieved December 9, 2003, from http://www.forbes.com/2001/04/26/eisner.html

Skymark.com. (2003). Walter Shewhart: the grandfather of total quality management. Retrieved January 29, 2004, from from http://www.skymark.com/resources/leaders/shewart.asp

Skymark.com. (2003). Joseph M. Juran. Retrieved January 29, 2004, from http://www.skymark.com/resources/leaders/juran.asp

Start a Campaign to Curb Runaway CEO Pay. Retrieved January, 2004, from http://www.aflcio.org/corporateamerica/paywatch/what2do/index.cfm

CHAPTER

NINE

Marketing: An Integral Part of

Management

Who are your customers? What do they want? How can you get them what they want? How can you reach them to let them know you have what they want? These are just some of the questions a corporation's leadership asks when forming a marketing strategy. Some companies seem to be geniuses at accomplishing branding their name and increasing their market share. Others are a little confused about who they are and, therefore, have a problem knowing who their customers are.

Introduction

In several instances, this book has shown that the information age is impacting corporate decision-making in a dynamic way. It has also shown that proper management of the new technological tools available is necessary, and that while technology is important, it is vital to maintain interpersonal communication for a business to survive. This book has also looked at how a company's financial integrity or lack thereof can mean the difference between success and failure. Another area that can mean success or failure for a company is its marketing.

Successful marketing management is a key element to any business endeavor. The philosophical attitude must stress customer satisfaction and the activities used must correspond with this philosophy. This chapter will discuss the marketing concept, strategic planning, market segmentation, global marketing, the marketing plan, and information systems. Several examples will illustrate the importance of marketing to a company's success.

The Marketing Concept

The marketing concept focuses on what customers want, integrating the organization's activities into satisfying the customer's needs. The marketing concept leads to achieving long-term goals for the organization legally and responsibly. The organization distinguishes its products from the competitor's offerings, and integrates all the organization's activities (including production) into satisfying the customer's needs, which achieves long-term goals. Wal-Mart stores have become the leading discount retailer utilizing the marketing concept. Wal-Mart focuses on what its customers want: everyday low prices, items always in stock, and cashiers always available. Sears Roebuck and Company is an example of a company not utilizing the marketing concept. It lost a lot of business to specialty stores and discount stores. Its competitors were doing a better job of satisfying customer's wants and needs. Sears CEO, Arthur C. Martinez, admitted not knowing who Sears wanted to serve, which was a huge hole in Sears' strategy (Lamb, Hair, & McDaniel, 1999).

Strategic Planning

Strategic planning is based on many individual attitudes within an organization, and in order to be effective, is interwoven with the organizational mission and objectives. Because the future of the business depends on planning, the entire population of the business must be familiar with the plan. This strategy depends on many factors, such as the competitor's strategy (Kotler, 1994).

Kmart is a troubled retailer that has had to change its strategic plan to adjust to Chapter 11 bankruptcy. It attempted to utilize a variety of initiatives, such as TV and video games, to increase customer loyalty. In 2002, Kmart developed a new product line with Martha Stewart as its headliner, advertising "The Stuff of Life" campaign that was directed by Spike Lee. Kmart utilized radio as well as billboards to improve its market (Cuneo, April, 2002).

In July 2002, Kmart's sales were continuing to plummet and it struggled to find a marketing strategy to pull it out of a deep hole. Martha Stewart, who had been Kmart's biggest asset, was now hurting the company, as her name was tarnished with allegations of insider trading. To change strategies, Kmart hired the Arnell Group from New York to help revamp the stores. The retailer was trying to find its niche between Wal-Mart and Target (Cuneo, July, 2002).

Though the Kmart name is a strong sell, many analysts believe there is not room for three major discount store chains. In 2003, the senior vice-president of Kmart's marketing department was terminated as the company struggled to reorganize its marketing department. This was said to be part of a corporate downsizing. With a new CEO, it is believed the senior vice-president of advertising will take over the duties of the senior vice-president for marketing. Though hundreds of stores have closed, the promotion "Savings Are Here to Stay" is being utilized to maintain loyal customers, with the Joe Boxer and Martha Stewart lines continuing to be its mainstays (AdAge.com, 2003).

A market niche is a firm that specializes in a specific market. It becomes specialized in some service, specific geographical area, product line, product feature, or quality or price level (Kotler, 1994). This is also an example of market segmentation, discussed later in this chapter.

An example of a niche is Hanna Anderson, a company that specializes in 100% cotton, washable clothing for kids. The company is known for excellent service, and has a policy that when a child has outgrown the clothing, the clothes can be returned for 20% off the next purchase (Boyd, Walker, Mullins, & Larreche, 2002).

The organizational mission and objectives are very important to marketing management and the strategies that marketing will undertake. These objectives must be communicated business wide. The marketing strategies may be constrained by corporate or business goals. They might impede sales growth, market share, and contribution margin, as well as customer satisfaction. Therefore, any issues that constrict marketing must be conveyed to the management (Boyd, et al., 2002).

An example of this is the marketing of tobacco and alcohol to teenagers. The uproar was heard across the globe when the Joe Camel icon was used in Camel cigarette advertising. Another example is "Alcopops" that are popular in Britain. The alcohol content is greater than that of beer and very tasty, with alcoholic lemonades, colas, and orange drinks available. Britain's Advertising Standards Authority banned a series of ads for Hooper's Hooch, which features a mischievous cartoon lemon. The critics claim these drinks induce underage drinking. Bass brewing contends these drinks are no more appealing to young people than other alcoholic beverages (Lamb, et al., 1999). These would also be examples of target marketing, according to the skeptics, although the companies deny the allegations. Ethical issues must be considered when looking at target marketing. Companies often face ethical problems because, for example, hospitals want only patients with insurance and credit card companies want people with good credit ratings, etc.

Market Segmentation and Target Marketing

Market segmentation is the process by which a market is divided into subsets of individuals who respond in similar ways to a particular offering or program because of similar needs and characteristics. Target marketing requires evaluating these subsets to determine which segments the firm wants to pursue. This entails evaluating market potential, growth rate, and the firm's mission and capabilities to create a unique image or position in the customer's mind. Because population growth has slowed and more product markets are maturing, there is more intense competition, which makes market segmentation increasingly important in developing marketing strategies (Lamb, et al., 1999).

An excellent example of segmentation done the right way is Blue Ribbon Sports, the company now known as Nike. Its founders observed that a portion of the population was not being served – the long distance runner. Blue Ribbon Sports had the knowledge and expertise to position its shoes as the shoes that would enhance the performance of the best runners, and then, by implication, anyone else who ran (Boyd, et al., 2002).

An example of segmentation done the wrong way is the Power Tools Division of the Black & Decker Corporation. At one time, Black and Decker was the world's largest producer of power tools. Black and Decker had three primary divisions: Professional-Industrial, Professional-Tradesmen, and Consumer (Dolan, 2001). The tools in each division were of varying strengths and cost, depending on the division. Black & Decker saw its market share diminish in the Professional-Tradesmen division. Black & Decker conducted market research to determine the cause for the reduced sales and market loss. The problem was that the household products introduced into the market for consumers led the professional contractors to believe that the strength of all Black & Decker equipment was that of a household product. In addition, there was not enough difference in appearance to distinguish the Professional-Tradesmen products from the household products (Dolan, 2001).

Global Marketing

Examples of market segmentation may also be seen in the global marketplace. Global marketing is not just an alternative for big business; it is imperative for the survival of a thriving business. Even if a company is not considering going global, its competition may be from foreign countries. Over the past two decades, world trade has climbed from $200 billion to $7 trillion per year. Many of the major businesses in the United States rely on the majority of their revenue to come from international divisions. Traditionally, marketing globally has meant developing a marketing plan for each country or region based on the culture of that country. McDonald's is a great example of a multinational company. It changes its products to suit each individual country. For example, McDonald's offers beer in Germany, beer and mineral water in France, and sake in Japan (Lamb, et al., 1999).

Because of technological developments affecting communication, travel, and transportation, market segmentation may cross country borders. One example is termed lifestyle marketing and is based on the belief that lifestyles have merged across borders. Segmenting markets based on lifestyle provides a wide degree of flexibility. An example of this is the teenage segment. Because people of similar age, income, and education often differ in purchases, there have been many profiles developed by marketing research firms to measure consumer attitudes, values, sports, and fashion (Lamb, et al., 1999).

Nike designed a standardized global market plan for its Air 180 shoe. Its advertising consisted of commercials that were not narrated, but used title cards translated into different languages to promote worldwide availability. Proctor and Gamble modifies its products that are marketed similarly all over the world. Camay may smell differently, Crest may have a different taste, and the formula for Head and Shoulders may differ from country to country (Lamb, et al., 1999).

In today's market, the growing trend toward nationalist sentiments must not be overlooked. Many people have strong loyalties to their country and are offended by Western encroachment. An example of this occurred in India, where Hindu protestors smashed Pepsi bottles and burned Pepsi posters in the country's first Kentucky Fried Chicken (Boyd, et al., 2002). The décor of this restaurant was a huge mistake and research was not done as to the culture of the country. Similarly, now would not be a good time to put an American restaurant with obvious American symbolism in Baghdad. However, it would it be a good time to invest in the growth of Iraq with a restaurant run by the Iraqi people, with proper research done on the wants and needs of the Iraqi people.

Marketing Plan

Developing a written plan is imperative because it spells out what actions must be taken, as well as who will do them and when they will be done. This ensures effective execution of the strategic marketing program. It is considered the benchmark for the entire organization and therefore must be approved by the management. Success depends on communication throughout the organization, with cooperation from the entire staff and all departments (Boyd, et al., 2002).

Information Systems

Certainly, the chapter "Technology: Management for Effective Communication and Decision Making" provides insight to the importance of information technology. The lifeblood of marketing decisions is accurate and timely information. An information system is critical in preparing and adjusting marketing plans and for gathering "market intelligence." One such system is called a marketing decision support system (DSS). Characteristics important to a DSS are that it is interactive, flexible, discovery-oriented, and accessible. Interactive indicates that simple instructions give immediate results; for example, no waiting for reports. Flexibility is required to sort, regroup, and manipulate data. Marketing intelligence is gathered by probing for trends and isolating problems using the DSS system. The DSS is easy to learn, yet it has advanced features that can be gradually learned (Lamb, et al., 1999).

The computer revolution and technological advances are changing the nature of marketing management. An example of excellent utilization is Fingerhut. Fingerhut tracks the purchases of individuals and personalizes catalogs to be sent to them. This can help a firm identify and target potential customers. These advances have helped businesses communicate throughout their organizations, as well as communicate efficiently with suppliers and distributors (Boyd, et al., 2002).

<u>Conclusion</u>

This chapter has focused on the basics of marketing management. In doing so, it has discussed companies that have succeeded and those that have failed. Certainly, the well-organized marketing management system that includes a written marketing plan can help assure the success of a company that is faltering. This cannot be done without developing a strategic plan for the organization.

References

Adage.com. Kmart's top marketing officer sacked; Steve Feuling managed TV advertising campaigns. Retrieved August 9, 2003, from www.adage.com/news.cms?newsId=37381

Boyd, H., Walker, O., Mullins, J., & Larreche, J. (2002). *Marketing management: a strategic decision-making approach.* New York: McGraw- Hill/Irwin.

Cuneo, A. (April 29, 2002). Kmart Hires CAA for Entertainment Strategies. Retrieved from www.adage.com/news.cms?newsId=34586

Cuneo, A. (July 29, 2002). Kmart Struggles to Find Effective Marketing Strategy. Retrieved from www.adage.com/news.cms?newsId=35585

Dolan, R. (2001). *The Black & Decker Corporation (A): power tools division.* MA: Harvard Business School Publishing.

Kotler, P. (1994). *Marketing management (8ᵗʰ ed.).* New Jersey: Prentice-Hall, Inc.

Lamb, C., Hair, J., & McDaniel, C. (1999). *Essentials of marketing.* Ohio: South-Western College Publishing.

CHAPTER

TEN

Multi-National Corporations:

Understanding Global Operations

Is your company thinking of going global? If it has not, it probably needs to if it wants to remain competitive. The future is globalization. More trade barriers are removed every year. Competition is coming. Not just from within the United States, but also from outside its borders. In this chapter you will find the options for going global and some problems that might be encountered, as well as a couple of companies from which good examples can be learned.

Introduction

The corporate playing field is becoming increasingly global. For this reason, it is imperative that the management of an organization understands the complexities and risks of operating internationally. Cultural differences test the flexibility and diversity of corporations seeking to break into the global marketplace. Global treaties are opening doors for more unfettered global trade while challenging the traditional sovereignty of national economies. Ideas of a global standard for business ethics are beginning to emerge. Until these standards are finalized, though, differing ethical standards will continue to challenge global operations.

It is increasingly necessary for organizations to expand internationally in order to maintain competitive advantage. However, some corporations have not had success in doing so and it is imperative that managers understand why companies have trouble in global endeavors.

This chapter will explore multinational corporations and the problems they face when dealing with the climate of the global community. Multinational corporations are structured in many ways, which will be outlined in this chapter. Examples will be given to help gain an understanding of the mistakes that can be made and the crises corporations can face when breaking into the global marketplace.

Multinational Corporations

The multinational corporation is easily defined as any corporation that does business outside of its national borders. Some countries, however, classify a company as multinational only if it generates a predefined percentage of its sales from business outside its national borders. The following paragraphs will explain some of the different ways in which a multinational corporation might develop its operations.

Multinational corporations can arise from export activities, wherein a company attempts to break into a new market by manufacturing a product and exporting it to another country for resale. A significant factor to consider when deciding to follow an exporting model of business is whether or not the product to be exported is 'transferable' to the foreign location. "A cross-border, cross-function product-development process is the international organizational capability needed by the exporting firm" (Galbraith, 2000, p. 31).

Governments may at times impose high tariffs on imports or refuse to allow imports of certain items altogether, making it necessary for a corporation to enter into a licensing agreement with a foreign producer. In that case, only the knowledge or technology of the corporation is actually being used internationally:

> The most common reasons for a licensor to enter into a licensing agreement are to benefit from the better manufacturing capacity, wider distribution outlets, greater local knowledge and management expertise of the licensee. Therefore, the licensor may, through the licensee, expand into markets more effectively and with greater ease than would have been possible if he had tried to do so on his own. The licensee will benefit from superior technology enabling it to produce better-quality products, or cut costs and improve efficiency. (Nanayakkara, 2002, p. 13)

Yet another way that a corporation might deal internationally is to enter into a joint venture with a similar type of foreign company. Having a close partnership like this reduces political risk because "the foreign companies generally bring new technologies and business practices into the joint venture, while the domestic companies already have the relationships and requisite governmental documents within the country along with being entrenched in the domestic industry" (Legal Information Institute, 2003).

One corporation that utilizes joint ventures quite extensively is Nokia. "Regional joint ventures have proven to be an effective way to combine Nokia's global technology leadership with strong local partners to accomplish faster and higher market penetration in new and emerging markets" (Nokia.com, 2004). For more information about Nokia and its operations, you can visit its Web site at http://www.nokia.com.

Joint ventures are also used when the products of a company cannot be sufficiently 'transferred,' or adapted, to meet the needs or lifestyles of a foreign company. McDonald's, for instance, has had to "recreate its supply chain" in other countries, and "it has developed an international partnering capability" (Galbraith, 2000, p. 32-33).

The most hazardous, as well as potentially profitable of international dealings, is for a corporation to have a wholly owned foreign subsidiary. Corporations may choose to do this when there is not a local producer with sufficient knowledge, operating space, or capital to enter into a joint venture. In this case, there is a high political risk of the government freezing or seizing the subsidiary's assets in the event relationships between the host country's government and the parent company deteriorate.

Some accuse corporations of using subsidiaries to avoid their homeland taxes or to exploit technology, as well as to pay low wages and take advantage of the currency in foreign countries. For example:

> IRS data show that foreign-owned corporations doing business here typically pay far less in U.S. income taxes than do purely American firms with comparable sales and assets. The same loopholes that foreign companies use are also utilized by U.S. owned multinationals, and even provide incentives for American companies to move plants and jobs overseas (Citizens for Tax Justice, n.d.).

Cultural Concerns

Some cultures are more accepting of international business than others are. It would probably be a bad idea to open a Hard Rock Cafe in Baghdad, Iraq, given the current political climate. "The world continues to grow increasingly uneasy with Uncle Sam, whom some people see as the big bully in our global village" (Diuguid, 2000). American corporations need to understand this and make sure they are sensitive to cultural differences when opening their doors in a foreign country.

Many countries see the globalization, or indeed even the Americanization of business as a threat to their sovereign cultural identities. "Much of the world's cultural diversity is being destroyed through global assimilation" (Buchholz & Rosenthal, 2000, p. 130). Diuguid (2000) adds, "Already nearly a quarter of the human population, or 1.5 billion people, now speak English as their common language." This same fact can be a blessing to a multinational corporation seeking to do business in a country that welcomes Western technology and investment.

It is also important to recognize basic cultural consumer needs in differing foreign markets. GE found this out with its many attempts to enter various foreign markets. Bartlett and Ghoshal (1998, p.89) state, "New plants, transferred technology, and assigned-from-home managers did not compensate for the failure to understand local distribution, competition, regulations, and consumer preferences."

Governmental / Trade Relationships

Another dynamic to be explored for a company seeking to break into an international endeavor is the relationship with a host country's government. Many actions have been taken in the global community to lessen the possibility of trade problems among countries. One major organization is the World Trade Organization (WTO). The WTO was founded in 1995 but grew out of the former General Agreement on Tariffs and Trade (GATT), which had been in effect since the end of WWII. "The WTO's overriding objective is to help trade flow smoothly, freely, fairly, and predictably." (World Trade Organization, n.d.). The functions of the WTO are as follows:

- Administering trade agreements
- Acting as a forum for trade negotiations
- Settling trade disputes
- Reviewing national trade policies
- Assisting developing countries in trade policy issues through technical assistance and training programs
- Cooperating with other international organizations. (World Trade Organization, n.d.)

Since the WTO represents over 130 members who are 90% of the world's trade, and since it makes decisions by consensus of the member countries, it can be considered a very broad and effective operation in the global community.

Another trade agreement is the North American Free Trade Agreement. NAFTA is comprised of the United States of America, United Mexican States, and Canada. The stated objectives of NAFTA are as follows:

- Eliminate barriers to trade in, and facilitate the cross-border movement of, goods and services between the territories of the Parties;
- Promote conditions of fair competition in the free trade area;
- Increase substantially investment opportunities in the territories of the Parties;
- Provide adequate and effective protection and enforcement of intellectual property rights in each Party's territory;
- Create effective procedures for the implementation and application of this Agreement, for its joint administration and for the resolution of disputes; and
- Establish a framework for further trilateral, regional and multilateral cooperation to expand and enhance the benefits of this Agreement. (NAFTA, 2003)

NAFTA takes precedence over all parties' rights established in GATT in any areas of 'inconsistency.' It is also important to note that after nine years, opponents of NAFTA vehemently deny the "promised benefits of 200,000 new U.S. jobs from NAFTA per year, higher wages in Mexico and a growing U.S. trade surplus with Mexico, environmental cleanup and improved health along the border" (Public Citizen, 2003). In addition, after September 11, 2001, some even argue that this agreement has caused a breakdown of the United States border security.

There have been other agreements and treaties designed to open trade among nations. Latin America, Guatemala, Salvador, Honduras, and Nicaragua have signed CAMERE (Central American Economic Integration) and the Caribbean Community has signed CARICOM. Another is Mercosur, which is a Customs Union that got its start with the Argentina-Brazil Agreement on Integration in the 1980s. Various agreements concerning environmental affairs and intellectual property rights exist as well. All of these multiple trade agreements and treaties have served to blur national borders and open foreign markets to allow for less problematic dealings for parent corporations in foreign countries.

Global Ethics

Another major factor to discuss when electing to do business on a global level is the differing business ethics of countries and regions within the global community. An organization that does not take time to understand how matters will be resolved when it is immersed in financial dealings with other countries can be detrimental to the future of not only the financial manager's career, but also to the future of the whole organization. "Companies' managers are becoming aware of the risk of expensive legal entanglements caused by doing business with firms having lower ethical standards than their own" (Hoffman, Kamm, Frederick, & Petry, 1994, p. xiii).

Some unethical situations seen in recent history have included corporate corruption, environmental protection lapses, hostile takeovers, insider trading, low wages, tax evasion, and illegal child labor activities, to name a few. "Historically, corruption has been considered evident to some degree in most societies, but it is frequently perceived to be more endemic in underdeveloped nations" (Hoffman et al., 1994, p. 14). Some cultures, and therefore countries, experience more of these bad behaviors than others do. Some countries rarely even experience such problems at all. For example, "Chile is remarkably free from corruption in its official bureaucracy, and its administrators receive high praise from foreign executives for their professionalism" (Hoffman et al., p. 5).

Because modern democracy is spreading rapidly, many countries have recently begun moving business operations out of the government's hands and into private citizen's hands. This causes a reliance on private owner's honesty and integrity. At the same time, many would like to see business ethics move away from reliance on individual integrity and toward a reliance of written standards for global operations:

> Although individuals of high moral character are valued as employees, large international enterprises increasingly rely on written policies and institutional guidance mechanisms to assure that the actions of an individual, including highly placed executives, do not jeopardize the company's long-term interests and value standards. (Hoffman et al., 1994, p. 4)

Having these written standards in place would certainly take care of the problem of employees and executives claiming 'I didn't know any better' when corruption rears its ugly head. America's market economy relies heavily on standards of individual honor. However:

> It has been argued that a system based on egoism, competition, and the lack of a conscious coordination mechanism has no future when compared with socialism, which is based on cooperation, rationality, and coordination. In fact, the economic crisis during the 1970s led many to believe that the capitalist system was mortally wounded. (Hoffman et al., 1994, p. 46)

So far, capitalism has remained intact. The question still lingers, however, how capitalism will fare in less-developed nations. It can be argued that reliance on the individual character of the masses is more to be desired than relying on the individual character of a dictator.

Tribulations also arrive when the standards of one culture's ethics collide with the standards of another and a global standard does not exist to mediate. One such example was the difference between intellectual property rights in America and Japan. The Japanese believe that the inventions and ideas of people are the property of, and for the betterment of, the nation. America believes that what an individual invents and thinks belongs to that person alone, at least for a period of time. America's IBM and Japan's Fujitsu computer companies went head to head on this matter throughout the 1970s and early 1980s:

> A simple contrast of the intellectual property laws of the two countries elucidates the "right versus right" elements in this case. On balance, the protection of copyrights, patents, and trade secrets was looser in Japan than in the United States during the 1970s and early 1980s. For example, U.S. copyright protection extended for 50 years; Japanese protection lasted 20 years. Under Japanese law, the user of a copyrighted computer program could debug, upgrade, and even modify the program under certain circumstances. Trade secrets could be protected in the United States by both law and contract. In general, they were protected only by contractual arrangements in Japan. (Hoffman et al., 1994, p. 82)

It was not a matter of America or Japan being more ethical, it was simply a matter of differing cultural definitions. These types of situations outline the need for a global standard of business ethics. "There will eventually be a U.N. 'Code of Conduct on Transnational Corporations' adopted by the General Assembly in more or less its present shape and content" (Hoffman et al. ,1994, p. 165).

However, problems will arise if this code is not restricted to transnational business alone. A large percentage of people and nations will not welcome these ethics codes on both a public and individual basis as they are being proposed, because:

> A "global" code would apply to all enterprises, personnel, and countries--necessarily transcending variations in domestic folkways and mores. Such a global code would have to cope with differences, for example, in common, civil, Islamic (which does not recognize interest charges), and communist law systems. (Hoffman et al., 1994, p. 168)

It is important for the financial manager of an organization to recognize differing cultural ethical standards and to know the guidelines that are available. One would do well to research a given country's and/or culture's ethical guidelines before entering into any business dealings with that country. A culture's ethics stem from its conduct and moral mindset. For this reason, the multinational corporation cannot always expect its own ethics to harmonize with those of a foreign interest. However, when these ethical decisions do not compromise the morals of a multinational corporation in its home country, a middle ground may be found. The following sections present two examples of companies coping with multinational challenges.

Wal-Mart

Wal-Mart is a force with which to be reckoned. From its humble beginnings as a "small niche retailer in the South," (Evans, Stalk & Shulman, 1992) it has grown to become an American household name. Now, it is seeking to become a global household name. An article written in Harvard Business Review in 1992, which, at this point in history, can be seen as somewhat prophetic, says, "If Wal-Mart continues to gain market share at just one-half its historical rate, by 1995 the company will have eliminated all competitors from discount retailing with the exception of Kmart and Target" (Evans, Stalk & Shulman, 1992). While it may have taken a few more years, the truth of that statement is certainly being seen in today's retail marketplace.

Although it still has plenty of room to grow in the U.S., Wal-Mart has the foresight to recognize that, "Someday the U.S. will slow down, and international will be the growth vehicle for the company" (Dawley, Ihlwan, Shmidt, & Zellner, 2001). It is important that Wal-Mart understands that fact, because its endeavors into the international marketplace have not been without mistakes. These were mistakes that, without money and time, would probably have crippled a lesser corporation.

A huge setback for Wal-Mart, which resulted in an initial loss of $200 million in 2000, was its foray into Germany:

> Wal-Mart bought the 21 store Wertkauf hypermarket chain in 1997 and 74 unprofitable and often decrepit Interspar stores in 1998. Wal-Mart failed to understand Germany's retail culture, the regulations that can add five years or more to the launch of a new hypermarket, and the stiff competition among some 14 hypermarket chains in a stagnant market. (Dawley et al., 2001)

Wal-Mart thought it could do what had always worked in America without proper planning for the competition. After all, what does Wal-Mart know about competition?

Wal-Mart's experience in Germany was a lesson well learned when it bought the British chain ASDA in 1999 and found greater success by allowing the "country managers [to] handle their own buying, logistics, building design, and other operational decisions" (Dawley et al., 2001). In Japan, Wal-Mart has decided to take it slow with a joint venture. "It has taken an initial 6.1% stake in ailing food-and-clothing chain Seiyu Ltd., which it can raise to a controlling 33.4% … and to 66.7% by 2007. That gives Wal-Mart time to hone its strategy - or run for the exits" (Dawson, 2002).

Disney

Disney's initial failure with Euro-Disney is attributed almost solely to a lack of cultural assimilation. Because it had assumed most of the financial risk with the endeavor, Disney was hit hard when the cultures clashed. As a result, Disney:

> Made changes that honor the cultural codes of France: lower admissions prices, wine with lunch, and looser dress codes. Not surprisingly, today business there is brisker and Disneyland Paris is one of Europe's top destinations, as Disney continues to incorporate a multicultural perspective into its daily operations. (Stanoch, World Traveler Magazine)

If Disney overestimated the degree to which it would be welcomed in Europe, it made the opposite mistake in Japan. By licensing the construction and ownership of both of its parks in Japan to the Oriental Land Company, it has lost out on millions of revenues, even while pulling in $200 million in royalties and fees alone (Weber, 2002).

The executives of Disney hope to reverse both situations by opening Disney Hong Kong in the near future. Having already assimilated Disney media and merchandise into China, and with top executives such as CEO Michael Eisner making regular trips to China, Disney is well on its way to a successful endeavor (Weber, 2002). It is clear that corporations must do research in advance if they hope to gain the most out of their foreign endeavors.

<u>Conclusion</u>

This chapter has discussed information that needs to be considered and measured when a corporation seeks to develop multinational relations. It is essential for management to be able to define a multinational corporation and the levels at which they might operate. It is also necessary to understand the dynamics involved with working in a global climate. In addition, one needs to explore the subject of global business ethics in order to gain an understanding of the convolution of practices that a foreign country may introduce into the multinational corporation's operations.

Here are some questions that the management of a corporation might ask itself before starting business in a foreign country:

1. Have you selected good local partners?
2. Do your executives understand local traditions and speak the language?
3. Have you developed an organization that allows for strategic coordination across far-flung locations?
4. Have you earned the goodwill of citizens groups and government officials (Weber, 2002)?

The specific corporate examples provided here have hopefully given some insight into what can be learned from the mistakes and crises encountered by organizations that have already ventured into the global marketplace. In any endeavor, there are benefits and risks to be weighed. Nevertheless, the earlier a corporation researches and begins multinational dealings, the sooner it will be prepared for the competition of the emerging global community and the faster it will begin realizing the substantial advantages of international market diversification.

References

Bartlett, C. & Ghoshal, S. (1998). *Managing across borders: the transnational solution.* Boston, Mass: Harvard Business School Press.

Block, S. & Hirt, G. (2000). *Foundations of financial management.* Boston, Mass: Irwin McGraw-Hill.

Citizens for Tax Justice (CTJ). (n.d.). The hidden entitlements: 3 tax breaks for multinational corporations. Retrieved September, 2003, from http://www.ctj.org/hid_ent/part-2/part2-3.htm

Dawley, H., Ihlwan, M., Shmidt, K., & Zellner, W. (2001, September 3). How well does Wal-Mart travel? *Business Week.*

Dawson, C. (2002, April 1). Will Wal-Mart conquer Japan? *Business Week.* Retrieved September, 2003, from http://www.businessweek.com/magazine/content/02_13/b3776141.htm.

Diuguid, L. (9 August, 2000). Impact of America threatens world's diversity. Retrieved September, 2003, from http://www.commondreams.org/views/080900-101.htm

Evans, P., Shulman, L., & Stalk, G. (1992, March-April). Competing on capabilities: the new rules of corporate strategy. *Harvard Business Review.*

Galbraith, J. (2000). *Designing the global corporation.* San Francisco, CA: Jossey-Bass.

Hoffman, W., Kamm, J., Frederick, R., & Petry, E. (1994). *Emerging global business ethics.* Westport, CT: Quorum Books.

Legal Information Institute. (n.d.). Joint ventures: an overview. Retrieved September, 2003, from http://www.law.cornell.edu/topics/joint_ventures.html

NAFTA. (March 01, 2003). North American Free Trade Agreement. Retrieved September, 2003, from http://www.nafta-sec-alena.org/DefaultSite/legal/index_e.aspx?articleid=80.

Nanayakkara, T. (2002, April). Negotiating technology licensing agreements. *International Trade Forum,* 13. Retrieved February 6, 2004, from http://www.tradeforum.org/news/fullstory.php/aid/504/Negotiating_Technology_Licensing_Agreements.html

Nokia.com. (2004). Joint ventures. Retrieved February 6, 2004, from http://www.nokia.com/nokia/0,,33297,00.html

Political activist rejects award from shoe firm. (2002, August 2). *The Independent,* 16.

Public Citizen. (2003). North American Free Trade Agreement (NAFTA). Retrieved September, 2003 from http://www.citizen.org/trade/nafta/index.cfm

Rosenthal, S., & Buchholz, R. (2000). *Rethinking business ethics: a pragmatic approach.* New York: Oxford US.

Stanoch, P. (n.d.). When cultures clash. Reprinted with permission from Northwest Airlines "World Traveler Magazine." Retrieved September, 2003, from http://www.windowontheworldinc.com/pps_8.html

Weber, J. (Feb 2002). The ever-expanding, profit-maximizing, cultural-imperialist, wonderful world of Disney. Retrieved September, 2003, from http://www.wired.com/wired/archive/10.02/disney.html?pg=1&topic=&topic_set=

World Trade Organization. (n.d.). The WTO in brief: part 2 the organization. Retrieved February 6, 2004, from http://www.wto.org/english/thewto_e/whatis_e/inbrief_e/inbr02_e.ht

CHAPTER

ELEVEN

Enron: A Case Study in Strategic

Planning Failure

The history of capitalism will forever be tarnished with the shocking story of a company who committed almost every management blunder known to exist. The case study compiled here at the conclusion of this book was the inspiration for the theme of this book. A company's leadership could implement every good management procedure discussed thus far and still find itself in crisis if it does not do one thing and do it well. That one thing is strategic planning.

Only time will tell if Enron is the biggest scandal in corporate history. However, strong leadership and sound management will be the key to making sure your company is not listed in the hall of shame along with Enron.

Introduction

This book began with the emerging Information Revolution and the need to be ready for change. Many examples of success and failure in corporate management have been presented. Technology, communication, finance, ethics, human resources, leadership, marketing, global operations, and quality are all critical areas for management to focus on when seeking to avoid and even recover from crisis within a company. However, no discussion of the management of companies is complete without the exploration of strategic planning.

This book will close by examining a company that could have used a few lessons in strategy. This case study will explore Enron's climb to the pinnacle of success only to find itself in the depths of bankruptcy and ruin. Strategic tools that could have helped it recognize and recover from its crisis will be addressed as well. Anyone in a position of leadership can learn from Enron's mistakes and the strategic tools discussed within this chapter.

Enron is a company with a spectacular rise and even more spectacular fall. The world was asking: What happened? Why did it fail? What drove it to the top and then over the edge? Some people believe that it was greed, corporate scandal, and even mismanagement that contributed to the demise of Enron. While these were certainly factors, the root of its downfall was the lack of a consistent and long-term vision. Enron is a prime example of strategic failure.

How Enron Lost Its Vision

Enron, traded under the ticker symbol ENE, began its life with over 37,000 miles of natural gas pipeline. This was a direct result of the merger between Houston Natural Gas and InterNorth, a natural gas company based in Omaha, Nebraska. At its inception, Enron's vision was simple: *"To become the premiere natural gas pipeline in <u>North America</u>"* (Boje, 2002). To fully understand Enron, one must go back to 1911 and the creation of the Seven Sisters. The Supreme Court had just upheld the decisions of the lower courts and ordered the breakup of the Standard Oil monopoly run by John D. Rockefeller. With the breakup came the Seven Sisters – Exxon, Mobil, Shell, British Petroleum, Gulf, Texaco, and Chevron. Later, the merger of Exxon and Mobil left just six sisters, creating a void and leaving room for another. With the proper mix of time (70 years) and history (changing environment), Enron appeared (Boje, 2002).

In 1978, the Natural Gas Policy Act deregulated the natural gas market, reversing the gas shortages of the 1970's and dramatically reducing gas prices. In 1981, "Newly elected President Ronald Reagan imposes policy prescriptions as condition of support for World Bank, which includes privatization, deregulation of oil, gas and power markets to increase US access to non-OPEC sources of oil, and increase developing country debt service payments" (Boje, 2002). In 1984, "the Federal Energy Regulatory Commission issued Order Number 380, which declared that minimum bill contracts…were invalid"(Boje, 2002).

In 1984, conditions were perfect and Houston Natural Gas and InterNorth merged to form the Seventh Sister. HNG/InterNorth's first CEO was Kenneth Lay, who served years before at Exxon. Lay wanted change and the first thing he wanted to change was the HNG/InterNorth name. He wanted something more exciting, something people could quickly remember. The result was Enron, a name that has no meaning but that is easy to remember. In March 1986 the shareholders endorsed the name and Enron was truly born (Boje, 2002).

From the beginning, and through the years 1986–1990, Enron saw continued growth as the company expanded into its first overseas office in the United Kingdom. This growth was not without pain as Enron's first years were full of strife, beginning its life by withstanding corporate raiders and an international money laundering scandal. It was during this time that the auditing firm of Arthur Andersen was hired. Its findings were that two members of Enron's board had in fact laundered $130 million in oil trades through the Channel Islands for Enron. Its recommendation was to fire the two board members. Lay deferred and ordered that the two members be retained. In 1987, Lay finally fired the two Enron board members. In 1990, Enron formally filed a lawsuit in the District Court of New York, charging the former two employees for diverting the funds for personal use and benefit (Boje, 2002).

In 1990, despite this mixed success and strife, Lay decided that Enron needed a new mission. Enron's new mission became, *"To become the world's first natural gas major"*(Boje, 2002). During the period from 1992 to 1995, Enron continued to experience growth and chaos as it adopted market–to–market accounting, expanded its pipelines into South America, and added many notable names to its cast of employees. Jeffrey Skilling joined the company from the consulting group of McKinsey & Co., where he had been a senior partner. More importantly, he had worked on the files and been a consultant to Enron. Upon joining Enron, Skilling became the chairman of Enron Gas Services. From Continental Bank came Andrew Fastow to manage Enron Finance Corporation, later he CFO of Enron itself. The final significant addition was Rebecca Mark, know as "Mark the Shark." She became the CEO of the Enron Development Corporation (Boje, 2002).

It is suggested that during the next ten years Skilling and Mark engaged in a rivalry that would ultimately be the final undoing for Enron as they battled to upstage the other. Each escapade was a more grandiose and more expensive event than the one before (Boje, 2002). This turmoil came at a price, both in terms of economics and corporate harmony. The Enron vision seems to have gotten lost in the early days of the corporation and with a lack of sound leadership, it was not to be regained.

Within its operations, Enron continued to expand and nothing seemed to stop the continued growth, even though problems persisted. Enron's power plant in Dabhol, India was met with severe skepticism. Its plant, "the largest gas fired plant in the world…produced electricity that cost three times as much as its competitor's, and than six times more than the coal fired plant that it replaced" (Boje, 2002). Interestingly, from 1994 – 1998, the Clinton administration provided three loans to the Dabhol power project. Unfortunately, the Dubhol plant has subsequently gone out of business (Boje, 2002).

Following the conclusion of the Gulf War in 1993, Enron was awarded a questionable contract to rebuild the Kuwaiti Shuaiba power plant. The contract was questionable because several members of the Bush administration were involved in the effort to convince the Kuwait government to let Enron build the plant. The other side of the controversy centered on the price that Enron intended to charge for the power, it was significantly higher than the price proposed by competitors (Boje, 2002).

Enron continued to be surrounded by controversy. Wendy Gramm (who was the former "head of the Federal Energy Regulatory Commission"), who had been instrumental in "remov[ing] a number of exotic financial transactions from federal regulations" as the first Bush "administration's top commodities market regulator," joined the Enron Board of Directors (Boje, 2002). Additionally, several other members joined the Enron team as either consultants or as directors, including: the retired Secretary of State James Baker, Secretary of Commerce Robert Mosbacher, and the retired Secretary of State for Energy and the leader of the House of Lords, the Right Honorable Lord Wakeham (Boje, 2002).

Clearly, Enron was using every available trump card to propel itself forward and to satisfy its vision of being 'the world's first natural gas major.' Unfortunately, performance could not keep up with the vision, as Enron was forced to admit that it had been using one of its controlled subsidiaries, Enron Global Power & Pipeline, as "a dumping ground for troubled Enron projects and liabilities" (Boje, 2002). One of the projects, a Guatemalan power plant, was known for its "higher than projected downtime, and higher operating and maintenance costs" (Boje, 2002). Ironically, the Enron Global Power & Pipeline CRO was known to have "worked closely with Arthur Andersen and Vinson & Elkins LLP, (Enron's law firm)" in setting up its cost control procedures (Boje, 2002).

In 1994, Enron processed its first electricity trade. In 1995, it entered into the European wholesale market with Enron Europe. Enron once again changed its mission statement. Enron now wanted *"To become the world's leading energy company"*(Boje, 2002). Despite all of its troubles, Enron continued to grow. By 1996, it owned "$19 billion worth of power plants in over two dozen countries" and was touted as the "New Economy" company of the future (Boje, 2002). "Its strategy of downsizing and outsourcing employees" was seen as the "role model of the New Economy"(Boje, 2002). At that same time, Lay was quoted as saying, "I have a strong belief in markets. In fact, I think that an imperfect market is preferable to a perfect regulator" (qtd. in Boje, 2002).

The beginning of the downfall for Enron is hard to pin down but could be said to have started as early as 1997. Even though, in 1997, Enron was thriving. It was on the move, acquiring electric utility holding company Portland General Corp. for about $2 billion.

> By the end of that year, Skilling had developed the division by then known as Enron Capital and Trade Resources into the nation's largest wholesale buyer and seller of natural gas and electricity. Revenue grew to $7 billion from $2 billion, and the number of employees in the division skyrocketed to more than 2,000 from 200. (Thomas, 2002)

Another move came when Peco Energy, a large gas utility in Pennsylvania, offered to cut rates by 10 percent. Subsequently, Enron saw a chance to enter the market and launched a lobbying and public relations effort to promote its offer of a 20 percent discount (Boje, Durand, Luhman & Rosile, 2004). Enron won the contract:

> The day Peco filed its plan with regulators, Mr. Skilling got up at 4.30am and by 9am had done nine radio interviews. By noon, Enron had an airplane circling Peco's HQ in Philadelphia with a banner saying: 'Enron doubles Peco's rate cuts.' (qtd. in Boje, Durand, Luhman, & Rosile, 2004)

In 1999, Enron acquired the Wessex Water Company of Britain for $2.2 billion, which then established itself as a monopoly over the water supplies in much of southwest England. In the midst of all of this was a "secret partnership" called Chewco, which:

> Was a confidential partnership that Fastow's team concocted to keep more than $600 million in debt off Enron's books, keeping it hidden from analysts, average investors, and pesky regulators. Fastow assigned his top deputy, Michael J. Kopper, to own and manage Chewco (Boje, 2002). Because of these events, one can assume that Enron's financial facade was being propped up by these off-the-balance-sheet partnerships. (Boje, 2002)

During the next two years, Enron continued to expand. In 1999, Enron announced the launch of:

> Enron Online, its Internet-based system for wholesale energy trading. Enron Broadband Services introduced the Enron Intelligent Network (EIN), a new Internet application delivery platform. Enron Investment Partners [was] created to manage private equity funds targeting women and minority owned businesses in Houston and around the U.S. Enron and the Houston Astros announced the name of Houston's new ballpark, "Enron Field," and a 30-year facilities management contract with EES. The 826 MW Phase I of the Dabhol Power Project began commercial operation, and financing for the 1,624 MW Phase II and India's first LNG receiving facility was completed. EES transacted its first billion-dollar deal with Suiza Foods. (Boje, 2002)

Despite this continued growth, Enron could not shake the misdeeds and scandals that centered on it, including:

-   Skilling obtaining permission from the Enron Board of Directors to date an Enron secretary a woman whom insiders called "Va Voom" behind her back. The secretary was quickly promoted to the position of executive secretary to Enron's board of directors; and her salary was raised to $600,000.
-   The Human Rights Watch report that charged, "The Enron subsidiaries paid local law enforcement to suppress opposition to its power plant south of Bombay."
-   The Enron board of directors' audit committee gave a detailed presentation on Enron's accounting, saying it was "high risk" in several categories with a high probability their accounting techniques could be questioned.
-   Enron withdraws from oil and natural gas production with divestment of its remaining stake in subsidiary Enron Oil & Gas Co. which is renamed EOG Resources.

- Enron filed a public report on its financial results, disclosing that a senior executive was managing a partnership, LJM Cayman LP. The item, said Enron, had engaged in a series of complicated deals with LJM, including the transfer of 3.4 million shares of stock, then worth about $100 million.
- Enron switched brokers from Paine Webber to Merrill Lynch when Paine Webber states opposition to the LJM partnerships and urges investors to dump Enron stock.
- Treasurer Jeffrey McMahon approached Jeffrey K. Skilling with "serious concerns about Enron's dealings with the LJM partnerships. Also in March 2000, Kopper had invited Mordaunt to join in a confidential and secret investment deal, called Southampton Place that would take place when the LJM1 partnership was terminated. Southhampton bought out the interests of one of LJM1's principal investors, a British bank.
- Whistle Blowers inside Enron, who warned Enron upper executives that the LJM partnerships were a bad financial risk, were either dismissed or transferred. (Boje, 2002)

Ironically, in October 2000:

Fortune magazine named Enron "America's Most Innovative Company" for the fifth consecutive year; the top company for "Quality of Management;" and the second best company for "Employee Talent." In addition, Enron ranked in the top quarter of *Fortune*'s "Best 100 Companies to Work For in America" (qtd. in Boje, 2002). This was ironic because in November, "Enron's quarterly report disclosed that it had engaged in an array of transactions with the partnerships (Chewco, LJM1, and LJM2) for a total value of $1.2 billion. (Boje, 2002)

In late 2000, "wealthy Enron insiders systematically sold $1.1 billion worth of shares. However, when rumors began circulating that the company was in freefall, Enron executives responded by slapping no-sell restrictions on thousands of employees who wanted to unload their shares" (Boje, 2002).

In January 2001, Enron had a market value of more than $77 billion and its stock price was $82 per share. With all the controversy surrounding Enron, and the bubble about to burst, Enron made its final mission statement change: *"to become the World's Leading Company"* (Boje, 2002). At the end of 2001, in what can be seen as one of Lay's most despicable statements, he states, "I can honestly say I've never felt better about the company, its business model, its prospects, and probably most importantly our incredibly deep pool of talent" (qtd. in "Ruined By Enron," 2002). This was just after the CFO, Jeff Skilling, resigned and Lay had received a memo from an Enron accountant stating she was, "incredibly nervous that we will implode in a wave of accounting scandals" (qtd. in "Ruined by Enron," 2002).

Why Strategic Planning Was Needed For Recovery

To determine what happened to Enron requires an understanding of strategic planning. Enron's management either did not understand the implications of strategic planning, or it was disregarded in order to ensure short-term profits. A quick review of its mission statements gives a view of its lack of understanding:

- 1985 - To become the premier natural gas pipeline in *North America*
- 1990 - To become the *world's first natural gas major*
- 1995 - To become the *world's leading energy company*
- 2001 - To become the *world's leading company* (Boje, 2002).

Enron's strategic planning was fragmented at best. A successful organization must use a comprehensive strategic plan, which includes the following processes:

Strategic Planning involves making decisions about the organization's long-term goals and strategies. Strategic plans have a strong external orientation and cover major portions of the organization.

Strategic Goals are major targets or end results that relate to the long term survival, value, and growth of the organization. Top level managers usually establish goals that reflect both effectiveness (providing appropriate outputs) and efficiency (a high ratio of outputs to inputs). Typically strategic goals include various measures of return to shareholders, profitability, quantity and quality of outputs, market share, productivity, and contribution to society.

Strategy a pattern of actions and resource allocations designed to achieve goals of the organization.

Tactical Planning translates broad strategic goals and plans into specific goals and plans that are relevant to a definite portion of the organization, often a functional area like marketing or human resources.

Operational Planning identifies the specific procedures and processes required at lower levels of the organization. ("Strategic Planning," 2001)

Enron did not seem to have long-term goals or strategic goals. Indeed, as the conditions at Enron changed, so did the mission statement. Not once did Enron actually meet its stated mission, even though it had the assets to do so. Strategic planning requires that the strategic thinkers, the top layer of management, be responsible for the development and execution of the strategic plan. Enron did not have a consensus at the top. Most of the top managers, including Lay, Skilling, and others, seemed to be primarily concerned with continued expansion and personal profit without the formality of understanding and controlling Enron's growth. If the top layers of management had been interested, they could have used a balanced scorecard to reveal that they were failing, as shown in Figure 1.

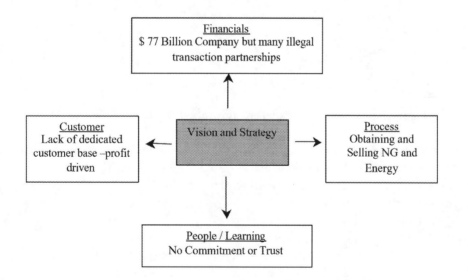

Figure 1. A balanced scorecard (Bateman & Snell, 2002)

The scorecard can be used by any organization's management to clarify the vision. Once the corporate scorecard is developed, business unit scorecards can be developed so that strategic goals can be translated into tactical and operation goals. Managers can conduct reviews of the business unit cards, which can help solidify or redefine the strategic plan. Finally, managers and employees can develop individual scorecards that link strategic and tactical plans to operational issues that are relevant to them. Annually, the company can conduct reviews and update strategies, which can then be used to clarify and reshape the overall strategy for the company (Bateman & Snell, 2002).

A comparison of Enron's strategic mission statement to one of its competitors would have also confirmed to upper management its lack of extended vision. Enron's statement "to become the world's first natural gas major" pales in comparison to Shell Oil Company's mission and vision statement, which reads:

> Shell Oil Company is in business to excel in the oil, gas petrochemical, and related business in the United States and where we add value internationally. In doing so, our mission is to maximize long-term shareholder value by being the best at meeting the expectations of customers, employees, suppliers, and the public. Our vision is to become the premiere U.S. Company with sustained world-class performance in all aspects of our business. (Bateman & Snell, 2002, p. 119-120)

The strategic management process is a series of six steps; each is a process in planning and using the decision-making process. This leads to formulating the long-term mission and vision of the company. As shown in Figure 2 (Bateman & Snell, 2002, p. 119), the process is rather specific.

A quick SWOT analysis by Enron could have determined several of the factors needed to provide a more accurate and attainable mission statement. For example, several factors can directly affect the mission and vision components of strategic management. The first factor is analysis of the external environment. This begins with the examination of the industry (oil and natural gas), the stakeholders (shareholders, banks, and creditors), the suppliers, the competitors

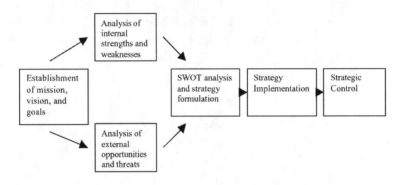

Figure 2. The strategic management process (Bateman & Snell, 2002)

(Exxon, Shell, Texaco, etc), the regulators (both government and business based), and others who are directly affected by the achievement of the organization's mission. The most critical task for the environmental analysis is forecasting future needs (Bateman & Snell, 2002, p. 121). Some of the activities involved in an environmental analysis are:

- industry and market analysis
    o industry profile, product lines and market segment
    o industry growth, growth rates for the entire industry
    o industry forces, threats from new or revised industry
- competitor analysis
    o competitor profile, major competitors
    o competitor analysis, goals, strategies of competitors
    o competitors advantages, product or cost leadership
- political and regulatory analysis
    o legislation or regulations
    o political activity
- social analysis
    o social issues and their effects on the industry
    o social interest groups
- human resources analysis

      o   labor issues
- macroeconomics analysis
      o   economic factors that affect supply and demand
- technological analysis
      o   technological methods that affect the industry. (Bateman & Snell, 2002, p.120)

During the process of reviewing an organization's external strengths and weaknesses, an internal analysis of strengths and weaknesses must also be conducted. This analysis should concentrate on functional areas within the organization. It should also provide management the means to assess the "organization's skills and resources, as well as its overall and functional performance levels" (Bateman & Snell, 2002, p. 122). An internal analysis should concentrate on the following areas:

- financial analysis, examines financial strengths weaknesses
- human resource assessment, examines strengths and weaknesses of all levels of management and employees concentrating on key human resources activities
- marketing audit, identifies markets, key market segments and the competitive position of the company
- operations analysis, examines the manufacturing, production or services areas of the company
- others, examines areas such as research and development, management information systems and purchasing. (Bateman & Snell, 2002, p. 123)

"Benchmarking is the process of assessing how well one company's basic functions and skills compare to those of other company or set of companies" (Bateman & Snell, 2002, p. 124). Enron could have used this to compare itself with its closest competitors. This could have led to direct questions such as: 1) Are our power plant prices competitive? 2) Do other successful oil companies do business on web-based systems or do they own and operate actual oil fields? 3) Do competitors create fake companies to buoy profits or to dump debt? Answers to these and other questions could have redefined or reversed Enron's course.

The next essential step in strategic management is a SWOT analysis. Again, a quick review by Enron could have determined several factors needed to provide a more accurate, attainable mission statement. For example, looking at some of the strengths, weaknesses, opportunities, and threats of Enron could have led management to see the problems that it was experiencing, and could have forecasted the long-term future in store for Enron. A SWOT analysis for Enron would look like the matrix shown in Figure 3.

Strengths	Weaknesses
- Corporate "Name" recognition - 37,000 miles of Pipeline - Political and Business connections - Sustained growth - Viewed as front runner in business	- Poor Management - Inability to rise above the temptations of fast money i.e. laundering, funds shifting
Opportunities	Threats
- Vast U.S. and World Markets - World need for their product - Innovative "New Economy"	- Political regulations - Foreign Competition - Poor Management Decisions - Moving too fast for financial resources - Questionable Accounting - Auditors

Figure 3: Enron SWOT Analysis

ENRON: A Summation

No company is destined to be doomed from the start, but without a long-term vision, ruin is almost inevitable. Enron did not have a complete mission statement and the one it had changed as often as the condition of the company. An analysis of its skills and capabilities would have been helpful as well. Enron seemed to never take a comprehensive review of itself and its competitors. Instead, it chose to plunge headlong into the natural gas and oil business with little or no regard for its financial future. Managers did not exercise the steps necessary to ensure the long-term survival of Enron. Instead, they chose to manipulate and deceive, while creating fatter and fatter bank accounts for themselves. Enron had the look and feel of the "New Economy," but underneath it was rotting to the core.

In the end, Enron's management team and its financial consultants (i.e. Arthur Andersen), found themselves facing bankruptcy, criminal charges, disbarment. Not only did Enron's management suffer consequences, its many employees were hurt as their jobs vanished, along with their pensions and 401k plans. Enron was never a success story; instead, it is a guide on how *not* to run a business.

Conclusion-Using Strategic Planning for Recovery

There are a myriad of possible solutions to the problems Enron faces, but few seem likely to benefit a company as broken as Enron. The answer for companies who wish to avoid this predicament, and who wish to recover from the crises they may face, is to do what Enron should have done all along – strategic planning, implementation, and control.

Bateman & Snell (2002, p.129-130) write that there are four steps to a successful business strategy:
- Define strategic tasks.
  - State what must be done to create or sustain a competitive advantage.
  - Define tasks in order to help employees understand how they contribute to the organization.
- Assess organization capabilities
  - Evaluate the organizations ability to implement the strategic plan.
- Develop implementation agenda
  - Management changes management pattern, determines what skills are needed in key roles, what structures, measures, information and rewards might support specified behavior. A philosophy statement is produced.
- Implementation plan
  - Management team, employee task force, and others develop the implementation plan.
  - Top management monitors progress
  - Employee task force provides feedback concerning how changes are being received.

After all of this is accomplished, strategic control (the final component of the strategic management process) is implemented. Strategic control is:

> Designed to support managers when evaluating the organization's progress with its strategy, and when discrepancies exist to take corrective action. The system must encourage efficient operations that are consistent with the overall plan while having the flexibility to adapt to changes. (Bateman & Snell, 2002, p. 130)

These steps to a successful business: define, assess, develop, implement, and control, are timeless. They are not to be done in the beginning and then forgotten about. Strategic planning can even be done daily, at least to a degree. However, it would never be a good idea to go more than a year without evaluating the strategic plan. When strategic planning is done and done correctly, any business can be run successfully.

As can be seen, Enron did indeed commit almost every management mistake a company could possibly make. The purpose of this book has been to explore the organizations that have failed to properly manage their operations. There are many reasons why a company might find itself in a crisis.

Management might fail to recognize change or proactively seek ways to change for the future. Companies could see technology as more of an expense than an asset and fail to plan for and maintain effective IT systems. Organizations often fail to focus on communication throughout the levels of management and across departments. Financial aspects, many times, allow for too much discretion and this can cause management to be tempted to be 'creative', which ultimately leads to crisis after the short-term gains are reaped. Crisis is also found when business leaders become too focused on profits and personal gain with no regard for ethics. Then, when a company is in crisis, it may tend to forget that the main assets it needs to recover are its human resources. Without them, the company may fail no matter what else it tries.

Companies also fall into a crisis situation when the leadership is flawed at upper levels. This can be seen when organizations implement lofty quality procedures yet still fall into disarray because of the poor quality upper management. Some corporations have wonderful products and/or services, but fail to implement sound marketing principles. Many organizations find themselves failing when they ignore the need to expand globally or when they do expand globally, but neglect to properly plan and research the expansion. Finally, crisis is found when companies disregard the one thing that should be the core of any business and that is: strategic planning.

Throughout this book these concepts have been outlined and discussed in-depth. It is obvious that there is much to be learned from businesses in crisis. Any person in corporate management must continually study good and bad management decisions that have been made in successful and failing organizations.

References

Boje, Ph.D., D. M. (2002). Enron chronology. Retrieved February 22, 2004, from http://cbae.nmsu.edu/~dboje/enron/chronology.htm

Boje, Ph.D., Durant, R.A., Luhman, J.T., & Rosile, G.A. Enron spectacle theatrics: a critical dramaturgical. Retrieved February 22, 2004, from http://cbae.nmsu.edu/~dboje/99/enron_spectacle_theatrics.htm

Bateman, T.S. & Snell, S.N. (2002). *Management: competing in the new era.* Boston: McGraw-Hill Irwin.

Ruined By Enron. (January 27, 2002). Retrieved from http://rwor.org/a/v23/1130-39/1136/enron_workers.htm

Thomas, W.C., CPA, PhD. (March/April, 2002). The rise and fall of Enron. Retrieved February 23, 2004 from http://www.aicpa.org/pubs/jofa/apr2002/thomas.htm

Strategic Planning. (March 26, 2001). A guide by NAVSEA Crane, Crane, Indiana. Unpublished document.

APPENDIX A:

Author Biographies

Sally Beth Acton RN, OCN

Employer

Schneck Medical Center

Oncology Department

411 W. Tipton St

Seymour, IN 47274

Title

Oncology Clinical Coordinator

Education

2004 Master of Science Management, Oakland City University

2000 Bachelor of Science, Organizational Management, Oakland City University

1979 Diploma Degree, Wishard Hospital School of Nursing

Biographical Data

Born in Seymour, Indiana, Sally graduated from Seymour High School. During her high school years, she began working at Schneck Medical Center as a candy striper and a nursing assistant, which paved the way for her to attend and graduate from Wishard Hospital School of Nursing. As a Registered Nurse, she worked in most of the areas in the hospital until 1986 when she found her calling with cancer patients. She continues to develop the Oncology Department as a Clinical Coordinator; she does patient care and also has a managerial role.

Married and the mother of two, she has been active in the community as a Girl Scout Leader, 4-H Leader, 4-H council president, American Cancer Society volunteer, and Psi Iota Xi Sorority President and Leadership, Jackson County.

In her position at Schneck Medical Center, she does extensive public and patient education, as well as staff education. She will utilize the MSM for management issues at the hospital and for teaching college level courses.

Jessica Alvarado

Employer

NSWC Crane

300 Highway 361

Crane, IN 47552

Title

Logistics Management Specialist

Education

2004 Master of Science Management, Oakland City University

2002 Bachelor of Science, Human Resource Management, Oakland City University

Biographical Data

Jessica Alvarado was born in Weslaco, Texas and at age 13 migrated with her family to the Midwest, where she and her family spent time working to make ends meet in agricultural farm work. Jessica's family then decided to stay in Syracuse, Indiana where she graduated from Wawasee High School in 1995. Only three months after graduation Jessica joined the Navy as an enlisted Hospital Corpsman and was stationed in Italy where she lived and worked for four years. Jessica held a number of assistant jobs in administration and patient health care. She returned to Indiana in 2000 to continue her education. In 2002, Jessica graduated with a B.S. in Human Resource Management. Jessica separated from the Navy after graduation and joined the civil service force Student Career Education Program continuing her long dedication to service for the Department of Defense. As a logistician in training, she supports the Naval fleet, works with quality assurance issues, and maintains a technical publication for fleet utilization. Jessica is also a certified facilitator for NSWC Crane in the "7 habits of highly effective people" workshop. She enjoys learning and decided to continue with MSM studies to further her knowledge and career.

Jessica spends her free time painting, writing and learning to play guitar.

Steven D. Booker

Employer

Technology Service Corporation (TSC)

116 W 6th St, Suite 200

Bloomington, IN 47402

Title

Quality Assurance

Education

2004 Master of Science Management, Oakland City University

2000 Bachelor of Science, General Studies, Indiana University

Biographical Data

Steve was born in Richmond, Indiana where he graduated high school in 1987. Steve moved to southern Indiana to attend Indiana University where he met his wife Natalie. They married in 1993 and reside in Bedford, Indiana.

Steve has worked at TSC since 1996. He has held a variety of positions, ranging from administrative assistant, computer network administrator, engineering support, and his current position of quality assurance. Among other things, this job entails proofreading and editing reports, delivering reports to the customer on time, and providing administrative support to the Southern Indiana Business Alliance. Prior to his current job, Steve has also held jobs in marketing, customer service, and training.

In his spare time, Steve enjoys his volunteer work with Big Brothers/Big Sisters, an organization with which he has been involved since 1996. Steve is also known to throw things up in the air and catch them repeatedly – he juggles balls, clubs, and fire (though not all at the same time). Finally, he has an eclectic hobby of collecting business cards; a collection that numbers over 50,000 cards.

Steve sought his Master's degree because he enjoys learning and knows the advanced degree will enhance his opportunities in the future.

Carl C. Caver

Employer
U.S. Navy
NSWC Crane
Crane, IN 47522

Title
Supervisor, Cryptologic Technician

Education

2004 Master of Science Management, Oakland City University

2003 Bachelor of Science, Organizational Management, Oakland City University

Biographical Data

Carl was born in San Diego, CA. Upon his father's discharge from the Navy in 1969, the family relocated to northern California. Carl graduated from Nevada Union High School in 1983. Later that year; based on a bet, a dare, and an unstable economy, Carl joined the Navy. His initial enlistment was only 4 years, long enough to receive some training, education, and to visit a few "exotic" countries.

2004 marked a memorable time in Carl's life, as it was the completion of his Master of Science in Management degree coinciding with the completion of this book. But most importantly, it was the completion of over 20 years of dedicated service in the Navy. These were not goals of his when he joined over 20 years ago, but when he realized that he was no longer "on the playground with the kid next door," he was determined to further educate and develop himself in order to be of greater value and service to society.

His wife Paige and three children Cody, Kyle, and Courtney, have always been an inspiration to him as he endured the many months away from home while serving in the Navy. During those final college years, his family was very understanding and patient, as it seemed like those late nights and long weekends working on those term papers and projects would never end for him and that the family outings for his children would never begin. With the closing of this chapter in Carl's life, he and his family move on to a new beginning, one that will finally allow them to put aside the nomadic lifestyle they have lived for so many years, one that is sure to provide more challenges but one that is sure to reap greater rewards.

Carl is a Cub Scout/Boy Scout Leader. In his spare time, he also enjoys restoring antique toys, coaching and participating in various sports, and woodworking.

Eugene Lewis Cottingham

Employer

Otis Elevator Company

1331 S. Curry Pike

Bloomington, IN 47401

Title

Consultant

Education

2004 Master of Science Management, Oakland City University

2003 Bachelor of Science, Organizational Management, Oakland City University (cum laude)

1994 Associate of Science, Business, Oakland City College (cum laude)

1987-90 Computer Studies, Ivy Tech

1971-72 General Studies, Indiana University

1971 Shoals High School, Shoals, IN (Salutatorian)

Biographical Data

Eugene Cottingham was born on February 3, 1953. He lived in Shoals, Indiana and went all twelve years of school there. It was in school that he met his future wife, Elaine. They were married July 22, 1972. In 1977, they had one son, Andrew. Andrew graduated from Indiana University in 2000, and is currently teaching for Lighthouse Christian Academy in Bloomington, Indiana. Eugene and Elaine presently live on a small farm in Martin County.

Eugene worked for Otis Elevator Company in Bloomington, Indiana beginning August 7, 1972. He has held several positions since he began, but has been a consultant in continuous improvement the last twelve years. In addition, during the past fourteen years, he has taught computer classes for Ivy Tech in Bloomington, Indiana. He was involved in retraining employees for Otis in 1990 when it underwent some downsizing. He was again involved in retraining Thomson Consumer Electronics' employees when it closed its factory in 1997. His career with Otis will probably come to an end in 2004 because Otis announced that manufacturing operations at the Bloomington plant will cease at the end of 2004.

Eugene pursued his education at Oakland City University for the past several years based on uncertainty in manufacturing. He hopes that his Master's degree will help him in choosing a new career.

Timothy R. Jones

Employer

Smithville Telephone Company, Inc.

1600 W. Temperance St

Ellettsville, IN 47429

Title

Corporate & Trust Accountant

Education

2004 Master of Science Management, Oakland City University

2001 Bachelor of Science, Accounting, University of Southern Indiana

Biographical Data

Tim Jones was born in the small town of Springville, Indiana in 1978, but held residence in Oolitic, Indiana for most of his childhood and school years. From there, Tim went on to graduate with honors from Bedford North Lawrence High School, leading him to choose University of Southern Indiana for his college career.

While in college, Tim established himself as a Founding Father of the Epsilon Gamma chapter of Alpha Sigma Phi fraternity at USI. While in the fraternity, Tim served as Treasurer and Vice-President, and was recognized as "Member of the Year 2000." He has called upon his experiences in the founding of this chapter many times in the everyday business world.

Tim's professional career started with Old National Bank while still in college. Upon graduation, Tim moved to the Accounting department of Shoe Carnival Corporation. Tim then decided to move forward with his career and accepted a position with Smithville Telephone.

Tim decided to enroll in OCU's Master's program to fulfill a life-long goal, while at the same time completing the 150-hour requirement to qualify for the CPA exam. Tim plans on using this degree to move forward with his professional career, with the hope of one day becoming CFO of a corporation.

Crystal Marie Kent

Employer

EG&G Technical Services

Bldg. # 64

Crane, IN 47522

Title

Accounting

Education

2004 Master of Science Management, Oakland City University

2002 Bachelor of Science, Accounting, Oakland City University

Biographical Data

Born in Indianapolis and raised in Ellettsville Indiana, Crystal attended Edgewood High School. She currently resides in Spencer, Indiana with her husband and three dogs.

Crystal began working when she was 15 years old. She has worked in retail, manufacturing, healthcare, and government environments gaining experience in sales, quality control, and accounting. She also runs a small home-based business doing marketing, advertising, and referrals for an 18-year-old Wellness Company.

A born-again Christian, Crystal is a member of South Union Christian Church in Bloomington, Indiana where she attends services, participates in bible studies, and volunteers as the Kid's Church Coordinator.

Crystal began to pursue the Master in Management to round off her education and broaden her opportunities for advancement within her career. She will have the necessary credits to sit for the CPA exam after obtaining the degree. Future aspirations include further career advancement, expansion of her home-based business, raising children, writing, and teaching part-time.

Jesse Mathew McCarthy

Employer

Wabash Foodservice

Vincennes, Indiana

Title

District Sales Manager

Education

2004 Master of Science Management, Oakland City University

2003 Bachelor of Science, Human Resource Management, Oakland City University

1988 Associate of Science, Business, Troy State University

1979 Jeffersonville High School, Jeffersonville Indiana

Biographical Data

Jesse McCarthy was born in Elizabethtown, Kentucky in June 1961. Upon completion of high school, Jesse joined the U.S. Army. During the next 20 years, Jesse was trained in two major areas. The first area was in the infantry, which accounted for 12 years of his enlistment. The second area was in recruiting, and was the last 8 years of his enlistment. The recruiting was the joy of his military career and is why he decided to continue his education in that area.

When Jesse retired from the U.S. Army, he realized that he was going to have to complete some education in order to be competitive in the job market. Jesse decided to attend Oakland City University to finish his degree to match his military education. Once Jesse started to go to school, the lessons seem to come easy to him, so when he had completed a Bachelor's degree he started on his Master's.

Jesse is married and has eight children, two of which have preceded him in death. Jesse has five grandchildren, one of which is currently living with him. Jesse's wife Athena is from Bloomington, Indiana and she is currently home schooling their grandson Shawn Rivera. Jesse and his grandson both enjoy NASCAR racing for a hobby. They have collected many items together and have enjoyed attending many races together.

Now that Jesse has completed the education that he started after, he is currently looking to return to the job that he loves the most, recruiting.

Michele Ann Murphy

Employer

Lawrence (County) Circuit Court

Guardian Ad Litem Program

1009 16th Street

Bedford, IN   47421

Title

Director, Lawrence Circuit Court Guardian Ad Litem Program

Education

2004 Master of Science Management, Oakland City University

1978 Bachelor of Science, Education Degree, University of Evansville

Biographical Data

Michele was born in Plymouth, Indiana. She graduated from Argos High School in 1974 and attended the University of Evansville in Evansville, Indiana. After graduating with a Bachelor of Science Degree in Education in 1978, Michele married and moved to Bedford, Indiana, where she still resides. Michele and her husband, Kevin, have two children; a son, Kyle, who recently graduated from Purdue University and now works as a mechanical engineer for Boeing, and a daughter, Meghan, who is currently attending Indiana University.

Michele worked as an educator in the public school system for several years before starting her own Daycare / Preschool business, which she operated for 12 years. Michele now works as the Director of the Lawrence Circuit Court Guardian Ad Litem Program, recruiting, training, and supervising volunteers who advocate for abused and neglected children. Michele serves on several committees that deal with issues relating to children. Michele enjoys working with children, reading, and traveling with her family.

Receiving her Master of Science in Management degree fulfills a lifetime goal and she hopes this accomplishment will help in the successful completion of her future career goals.

Kevin S. Suddeth

Employer

EG&G

300 Highway 361

Bldg 64

Crane. Indiana 47424

Title

Program Manager, Surface Electronics Warfare, Command, Comptroller, Management Systems and Supply Directorate Naval Surface Warfare Center (NSWC) Crane

Education

2004 Master of Science Management, Oakland City University

2003 Bachelor of Science in Organizational Management, Oakland City University

Biographical Data

Kevin is originally from central Illinois and graduated from Galesburg Senior High School in Galesburg, Illinois. Prior to high school graduation, Kevin married his high school sweetheart, Michelle. Shortly after high school, Kevin joined the US Navy in June of 1977 and spent the next twenty-three years seeing the world and serving his country as a Logistics Specialist. He served at various commands throughout the U.S. and overseas and onboard three ships; the USS Piedmont, the USS Butte, and the USS California. He has traveled throughout the various oceans and seas of the world including the Atlantic, Pacific, and Indian Oceans, as well as the Yellow, Mediterranean, and Caribbean Seas. He retired after serving the final three years of his career as the Command Senior Chief at NSWC Crane.

Michelle and Kevin have enjoyed over 27 years together, raised three children Stephanie Lee, Amanda Marie, and Jeramie Scott, and lived all over the world including Cherry Point, NC; Norfolk, VA; Keflavik, Iceland; Norman, OK; Bremerton, WA; and Bloomfield, IN.

Currently, Kevin is employed by EG&G Technical Services at NSWC Crane developing solutions by providing personnel requirements, work efforts, and technical leadership for over 55 task orders and 75 employees totaling over $15 million in business.

Kevin's hobbies include woodworking projects, sports cars, computers and the newest technological gadgets, along with spending time with his wife and family!

About The Authors

In 2002-2004, ten student came together to complete a Master of Science in Management degree from Oakland City University. As part of the program, they were required to complete a final project. The concept of a book discussing good and bad management decisions evolved, especially with class discussions about businesses caught in crisis; businesses like Enron, Arthur Andersen, Qwest, & Kmart.

The group wrote this book to help managers understand the importance of making sound decisions in daily business practices. Whether the topic be financial management. communication, marketing, or any other area of business, making good decisions is crucial to success. The authors hope the reader can learn from both the good and bad management decisions presented throughout the book.

Printed in the United States
By Bookmasters